MEDIA GENERATIONS

While the analysis of generations has been central in the sociological understanding of social change, the role of the media in this process has only been acknowledged as an important feature during the last couple of decades. Building on quantitative and qualitative comparative research, *Media Generations* analyses the role of the media in the formation of generational experience, identity and habitus, and how mediated nostalgia is an important part of the social formation of generations.

Avoiding popular generational labelling, Göran Bolin argues that the totality of the media landscape is a contextual structure that, together with age and life-course factors, help inform world views and ways to relate to the wider society that guide the actions of media users. *Media Generations* demonstrates how different generations come of age at different moments in the mediatised historical process, and not only develop different media habits, but also make sense of the world differently, which informs their relations to older and younger generations.

It also explores how this process of 'generationing', that is, the process in which a generation comes into being as a self-perceived social identity, partly builds on specific kinds of nostalgia that establish generational differences and distinctions. This book will be of special interest to those studying social change, collective memory, cultural identity and the role of the media in social experience.

Göran Bolin is Professor of Media and Communication Studies at Södertörn University, Stockholm, Sweden. He is the author of *Value and the Media: Cultural Production and Consumption in Digital Markets* (2011), and editor of *Cultural Technologies: The Shaping of Culture in Media and Society* (2012).

MEDIA GENERATIONS

Experience, identity and mediatised social change

Göran Bolin

 Routledge
Taylor & Francis Group

LONDON AND NEW YORK

First published 2017
by Routledge
2 Park Square, Milton Park, Abingdon, Oxon OX14 4RN

and by Routledge
711 Third Avenue, New York, NY 10017

Routledge is an imprint of the Taylor & Francis Group, an informa business

© 2017 Göran Bolin

British Library Cataloguing-in-Publication Data

A catalogue record for this book is available from the British Library

Library of Congress Cataloging-in-Publication Data
Names: Bolin, Göran, author.
Title: Media generations : experience, identity and mediatised social change/ Göran Bolin.
Description: London; New York : Routledge, 2016. | Includes bibliographicalreferences and index.
Identifiers: LCCN 2016002031| ISBN 9781138907676 (hbk) | ISBN 9781138907683(pbk) | ISBN 9781315694955 (ebk)
Subjects: LCSH: Mass media--Social aspects. | Mass media and culture. | Social change. | Population aging.
Classification: LCC HM1206 .B65 2016 | DDC 302.23--dc23
LC record available at http://lccn.loc.gov/
2016002031

ISBN: 978-1-138-90767-6 (hbk)
ISBN: 978-1-138-90768-3 (pbk)
ISBN: 978-1-315-69495-5 (ebk)

Typeset in Bembo
by Sunrise Setting Ltd, Brixham, UK

For generations to come

CONTENTS

LIST OF ILLUSTRATIONS

Figures

Tables

ACKNOWLEDGEMENTS

I have in various contexts presented earlier versions of the analyses in this book, and have benefitted from helpful comments from a wide range of scholars. I want to extend my deeply felt thanks to those who have specifically commented on previous versions of the analysis, discussed concepts and/or have provided me with interesting reading suggestions: Andra Siibak, Andreas Hepp, Anne Jerslev, Anne Kaun, Charles Ess, Chris Gilleard, Christina Ponte, Fausto Columbo, Galit Nimrod, Irena Reifová, Jakob Bjur, Joe Straubhaar, Johan Fornäs, Leopoldina Fortunati, Lisa Parks, Marta Cola, Nicoletta Vittadini, Piermarco Aroldi. Annette Hill, Mats Ekström, Rita Figueiras and Sakari Taipale have kindly invited me to their respective institutions in Lund, Gothenburg, Lisbon and Jyväskyle to present my work. I also learned much from being involved in COST Action ISO906 Transforming audiences, transforming societies, and especially the interest group on generations. To co edit a special issue of *Northern Lights* on 'Age, generation and the media' together with Eli Skogerbø was a rewarding experience that I learned a lot from, and besides Eli I want to thank all the contributing authors for that issue.

A special thanks to Signe Opermann who worked together with me to collect parts of the material, and whose valuable insights into Estonian language and culture the present analysis has benefitted enormously from. My uncle Anders Gahlin has provided me with the cover picture from his collection of family photos, for which he has my sincere thanks. I would also like to thank my mother Gurli Bolin for writing down her childhood memories, which I have used.

The funding for the research on which this book is based has been generously provided by the Foundation for Baltic and East European Studies. For ten years I also collaborated with the SOM Institute at Gothenburg University to collect survey data on mobile phone use, and I am very grateful for having had that opportunity to learn more about statistical analysis. Over these years I have had many interesting discussions with Oscar Westlund on generational uses of the mobile phone. Lastly, I want to thank my institutional colleagues at Södertörn University, for providing me with such an excellent research context.

Some sections of this book have been published earlier, and I want to thank the publishers of those journals for letting me reuse this material. Some parts of the analysis of mobile phone use in Sweden and Estonia in Chapter 3 were published as 'Domesticating the Mobile in Estonia' in *New Media & Society*, 12(1): 55-73 (2010). Parts of the analysis in Chapters 3 and 4 was first tried out in 'Media Generations: Objective and Subjective Media Landscapes and Nostalgia among Generations of Media Users', *Participations,* 11(2): 108-31 (2014). In Chapter 5 I have used parts of the analysis from 'Passion and Nostalgia in Generational Media Experiences', published in *European Journal of Cultural Studies (Online first)* (2015).

My last thanks go to my own private successors in the generation order, my daughters Lisa, Vera, Rut, Mina and Marta, to whom I dedicate this book.

INTRODUCTION

My mother was born in 1933. In those days, there were plenty of cinemas in the inner city of Stockholm, the city in which she was born and raised (also the city in which I live, and have spent the better part of my life). Cinema tickets were less expensive compared to the prices of today, and to working-class and lower middle-class families, living in small apartments, the cinema was a cheap form of pastime and entertainment. My grandfather was a keen cinemagoer, more so than my grandmother, and he often took my mother to the cinema, weekdays and weekends alike.

When my mother was five years old, her father took her to the local cinema to watch Disney's *Snow White and the Seven Dwarfs* (1937, Swedish premiere 1938). *Snow White* was the first animated full-length feature film, and my mother often recounted how that event had made a lasting impression on her. When I was a young boy, and the Swedish television showed a short clip from *Snow White* each Christmas Eve, my mother retold the story of how one specific scene had forever been imprinted in her mind: Snow White was running through the woods to escape the hunter sent out by the evil queen/stepmother, and the trees were reaching out to capture her. However, I could not share that experience with her as my only access to Disney's film was through the yearly clip of Snow White dancing with the seven dwarves, among whom she was hiding from the evil Queen, and – subsequently – the witch being chased to the top of a hill, where lightning struck her (in itself quite dramatic).

When my oldest daughter had reached the same age at which my mother saw *Snow White*, video had been firmly established in Sweden. In fact, to my oldest daughter, video has always been there – it is a given in the media environment for her. When the economic advantages of this new medium had been realised, Disney soon re-launched its classic back catalogue, and accordingly *Snow White* had a video sales premiere in 1994. Hence, my eldest daughter could – and did – watch the film at the same age as her grandmother had been when she first saw it, and could in fact share the traumatic experience with her (despite the different reception contexts), keeping me outside of their common experience. Quite naturally, I sat beside my daughter when she watched the film for the first time, but I was watching it through the experience of a male, thirty-something PhD candidate in Media and Communication Studies, backed up by an MA in Cinema Studies, which is a quite different life situation than that of a five-year-old girl.

In my family tree, my mother, my daughter, and myself represent three generations. We are united by the succession order of the family. We share a family history that is transferred over generations, mediated via family photo albums, Double-8 and Super-8 amateur film, and occasional tape recordings from festive occasions. This is generation by kinship. It is diachronic in nature, and it is very often represented in family albums through the three-generational line-up – as on the front cover of this book. The photo shows my mother Gurli in the summer of 1939. In this year she was six years old (that is, about a year after the encounter with *Snow White*). She is pictured together with her mother Dagny (my grandmother) and her grandmother Karin (my great-grandmother). If my mother was six at the time, then my grandmother, standing behind Karin, was 37, since she was born in 1902, and my great-grandmother was 61 (she was born in 1878). My grandfather Evert is also in the photo, as is my mother's aunt Ingeborg.

The photo is not only a representation of my family tree, it is also a time capsule that brings us back to another age – one that most of us have not experienced firsthand, but only experienced in mediated form. In the photo, my great-grandmother is just a few years older than I am at the time of writing. However, despite the fact that we share approximately the same age, there is very little else that we have in common when it comes to experiences gained over the five to six decades that we have walked this earth. For one, although I am a father, I do not yet have grandchildren. And although I have five children, a number that would seem quite high by today's standards, my great-grandmother gave birth to thirteen children over the course of 26 years, from 1896 to 1922. Added to that is the sex and gender difference, where, besides the fact that I cannot experience childbirth in the same way as she, no matter how engaged I would have been during the birthing process, the social (and societal) expectations on us have been dramatically different. Other important differences are our very different socio-economic conditions, our different education, the fact that she grew up in the rural countryside in the north of Sweden, while I grew up in Stockholm, and so on. So, although kin relates us, we share very few experiences, and in fact my great-grandmother probably shared more experiences with her contemporaries – people from her generation – than she would have done with me, had she lived.

As these differences reveal that generational kinship is not the only aspect of generation. There are also others, such as the synchronic generational relations between peers born around the same time (and within roughly the same national or geo-political space), having experienced similar events, and having been confronted with a similar cultural environment, including a similar media landscape.

These are social generations that are defined in relation to their contemporary peers, rather than in relation to kin.

In public and semi-academic discourse, the concept of generation is widely used, but these uses are most often found in popular accounts, where the concept of generation is sometimes reduced to a buzzword, and hence stripped of explanatory power. Such buzzwords include the 'net generation' (Tapscott 1998), the 'digital natives' (Prensky 2001), 'generation X' (Coupland 1991). These uses of the concept of generation have also met with a fair amount of criticism (e.g. Aroldi and Colombo 2013). However, not all labels are stripped of academic theorising. Thus, the concept of 'digital generation' has been discussed by Edmunds and Turner (2005), and Buckingham and Willett (2006), just as the Google generation (Gunter et al. 2009), with the ambition to theoretically pin down the specificities of those cohorts that grew up in a digitised world. Colombo and Fortunati (2011) have, with the same ambitions, theorised 'broadband generations', while Hartmann (2003) has sceptically deconstructed the concept of a 'web generation'.

Generation is also a concept that is used in relation to technology, the succession of technological standards and technological development. In the days of video recording, generation was used among video collectors and networks of film swappers to indicate the quality of a feature-film copy. To have a fourth generation copy meant poor quality because it indicated that the specific title was a copy of a copy of a copy of a copy of the original film as it was released from the distributor. For every generation, quality decreased, no matter how good your equipment was. Today, nobody makes copies of films in this way and the loss of quality is minimal with digital reproduction. Accordingly, no one speaks of a fourth generation digital copy. Since digital copies are exactly the same and it cannot be distinguished which one is the older, a generational differentiation is pointless because the concept of generation is relational.

In addition to these uses, generation is frequently used to refer to advances in technology; for example, when a more refined version of something becomes available, such as a type of computer game (Jenkins 2006a: 23) or a mobile phone. Most familiar will probably be the 3G technology of mobile phones. Just as 3G replaced the 2G phones, in turn replacing 1G technology, 3G has now been replaced by 4G. When it comes to mobile phone generations, there are rules set by the International Telecommunications Union (ITU), which prescribe that 4G should have certain speed requirements (at least 100 megabits per second for mobile units, and at least 1 gigabyte for stationary systems), and although the ITU does not have judicial authority, they have defining power as a reference point for the global telecommunications industries. With computers, generations are defined by the technological exchanges from vacuum tubes to transistors and integrated circuits, and to micro-processors. However, these technological generations are not the main concern here, although technological development sometimes also has an impact on how generations are defined, as seen from the examples of 'net generation' and 'digital generation'.

An additional use of the generation concept relates to migrants, and migrant families. In everyday parlance, first and second generation immigrants are common conceptions. However, these everyday expressions also point to some of the problems that stem from adding yet another generational layer to the already problematic conflation of generation as kinship and generation as social experience (Cola 2014). Being a 'first generation immigrant' is only restricted to the reference of being the first in one's family to have arrived in a new country, and hence all first generation immigrants share this feature irrespective of all other experiences, including those related to media, year of birth, societal events, and so on. In the body of research on immigrants' media use, generation is accordingly most often downplayed in the analysis, despite the common parlance in terms of immigrant generations, in favour of a focus on the media use of immigrants (e.g. Dhoest 2015, Dhoest et al. 2013, Vittadini et al. 2013a).

So, there is a growing popularity of generation as a concept – both in general public discourse and essayistic writings on the media and their users, and in more academic analyses. However, even if we restrict our discussion to the social dimension of the academic discourse, we need to explain the increased interest in generational theory. Clearly, interest arises because there are some benefits to this perspective, that are either intuitively felt or analytically arrived at. But what are the benefits of the generational perspective? It will be argued here that adopting a generational perspective on the study of media, culture and society is justified because it helps explain societal change by bridging objectivist and subjectivist analytical positions – a way of solving the structure/agency problemat in the social and human sciences. As will be explained more fully below, the generational perspective deals with both the objective conditions for acting in the world and for the perceptions of these structures. As these perceptions and experiences will vary depending on where and when they are perceived, they will also have an impact on the structural conditions. Taking the generation concept seriously and developing a well-theorised model for analysis based on the concept of generation is thus a tool for studying social and cultural change.

This book is about generations. More specifically, it is a book that discusses the role of the media in and for generations of media users: the ways in which the media are used by different generations and thus become defining for these generations, and also how the media help shape generations through their affordances. It takes as its point of departure the idea that the media are becoming an increasingly important feature in the experience of generations, and that the media – as technologies, content structures and communication modes – in some instances are the formative components in some generations. The example with my own mother and daughter, and how the media helped create an inter-generational bond that could connect them through a common experience, is but one aspect of this relation. In addition, there are many other ways in which the media affect generations across time, and across geographic and cultural distance.

The aim of this book is to critically examine this 'problem of media and generations', to paraphrase Mannheim, and to contribute to a theory of media and generations (maybe even of 'media generations'), as well as to the growing literature on generations more generally.

In Chapter 1, I will lay out some of the aspects of generation theory, and the ways in which research on generations has been conducted up until now. I will do so in order to discuss the theoretical and methodological underpinnings of the argument in more detail in the chapters to follow. Based on a review of the main literature in the field, I will introduce the ways in which the media as organisations and content structures might influence how generational identities are formed, and I will also examine the ways in which wider societal experiences inform media use and habit. As one of my main arguments throughout the book is that generations are defined both in relation to other generations that have preceded or succeeded them, that is, in relation to time, *and* to generations formed in other spatial contexts, I will discuss how comparative perspectives can inform our understanding of the process of generational formation. Since I will argue that generations are formed over time (and in relation to space), I will also relate the theory of generations to the mediatisation process; that is, the process by which media technologies and content have become increasingly more important components in everyday life, and hence also in the process of generation formation.

In Chapter 2, I will discuss in more detail how concepts such as age, birth cohorts, generation and life course interrelate. The basic argument of this chapter is that some features related to social (and also biological) age will have consequences for how our subjective and collective identities are formed, and will therefore also be important for the formation of a generational identity – especially if they are shared across broader birth cohorts, that is, by people born around the same time. The same goes for life-course perspectives that can help us understand why certain habits and modes of media use develop and mould with the generational experience. This chapter will also discuss how these concepts (and the theoretical models for explanation that are attached to them) appear in previous research; this will be used as a basis for the formulation of an analytical model that can then be used for a more empirically founded understanding of the role of media in the formation of generational experiences.

The following three chapters will then engage in an analysis of the role of the media in the formation of generations. Chapter 3 will discuss how certain birth cohorts, located at the same period in the general historical process, react to the social and media landscape that they grow up in. The concept of *landscape* as an 'objective' structure of media technology and content is used here to explain the context in which certain generational habits are formed, and how such habits can be analysed empirically at specific points in time and in relation to specific geo-social and geo-political contexts. The idea is to show how birth cohorts in neighbouring countries such as Sweden and Estonia developed different understandings, and hence self-perceptions, as a consequence of social, political, economic and technological differences over the twentieth century. One point is thus to show that generational experiences are always situated both in time and space, and the different locations of these cohorts produces different understandings among individuals in a way that also produces differences in collectively shared experiences.

In Chapter 4, these experiences are further analysed qualitatively in an attempt to try to grasp generational self-perceptions and generational experiences as they are subjectively perceived of in relation to a surrounding social and media landscape. This chapter will take as its empirical focus a series of focus-group interviews with people from different birth cohorts in Sweden and Estonia in order to try to understand the points at which they share common experiences, and at what points their experiences are marked by the specific national and historic location of the respective birth cohorts. The chapter will also briefly discuss the 'generationing' process: that is, the way in which a generational experience is not automatically formed in the meeting between a social group of cohort members and a surrounding social and media reality, but how a generational self-understanding is developed as a kind of narrative over time.

Chapter 5 will focus on nostalgia as one special feature of utmost importance for the generationing process. Nostalgia as a specific form of memory is here seen as related to, on the one hand, one's first childhood memories, and, on the other, memories from one's formative years in youth. While childhood memories are highly individual, they form a background of temporal situatedness that is then further established through collective experiences in the formative years of youth.

Chapter 6 will then summarise the empirical results and the discussion from the previous chapters. It will then more theoretically discuss generationing as an act of becoming, and the way in which this process relates to historical change. Here, generationing is explained in terms of a successively elaborated master narrative, resulting in an overarching story or fabula where the course of life (the syuzhet) is ordered into a comprehensive and linear life history, and where memory formation is of central concern. This chapter also relates the process of generationing to the mediatisation process as situated in the overarching matrix of modernity. This is also where the discussion on the concept of media generations is conducted.

1

THE PROBLEM OF MEDIA
AND GENERATIONS

In the wake of the First World War, and against its background of mass slaughter, industrialised warfare and the suffering of millions of citizens of Europe and beyond, sociologists such as Karl Mannheim (1928/1952) and philosophers like José Ortega y Gasset (1923/1931, 1930/1932) sought explanations for social change in the continuous exchanges of generations. Their aim was to unveil 'the rhythm of ages', as Ortega y Gasset (1923/1931: 18) poetically put it, and to use the concept of generation to understand the 'dynamic compromise between mass and individual' (p. 15). Of these two scholars, Mannheim was the theoretically most rigorous, and his ideas on how generations come into being have since inspired a range of sociological analyses. Many of these studies have concerned themselves with youth. Some have focused on how youths have become integrated into society (e.g. Eisenstadt 1956 and 1988, Kerzer 1983), while others have studied how and in what ways they have resisted such integration (e.g. Murdock and McCron 1976, Frith 1978). Some have looked at youth cultures from a perspective of movements (e.g. Jamison & Eyerman 1994, Eyerman & Turner 1998, Wyatt 1993), while others have sought to theoretically advance the generational theory more generally (e.g. Corsten 1999, Burnett 2010, Pilcher 1998, Vincent 2005). Irrespective of the approach taken, the sociological focus has emphasised the role of experience in the formation of generations, especially experiences of dynamic and revolutionary historical events such as war, famine or natural disaster, but also political upheaval, or state or military suppression. All of these dramatic types of events are supposed to have an impact on people's lives to the extent that the events are formative for the groups of people that experience them: they become central components in the everyday experience of living in modernity.

In these sociological accounts of generations, some components in people's lives seem to have attracted more attention than others. However, and despite the central place of media technologies and content in people's lives, generational theory has only recently been a prominent feature in media research, barring a few examples (e.g. Gumpert and Cathcart 1985, Bolin 1997, Hartmann 2003). Lately, however, we have seen a growing interest in generational components as part of media and audience research, where a few edited collections have dealt with the role of media in the formation of generations (Volkmer 2006a, Colombo & Fortunati 2011, Loos et al. 2012, Aroldi & Ponte 2012, Bolin & Skogerbø 2013, Vittadini et al., 2013b). The increased presence of the media in peoples' lives and in society more generally over the past century has also left few traces in the sociological literature on generations. This part of social and cultural development, which is sometimes referred to as the process of mediatisation (Krotz 2001, Lundby 2008, Hjarvard 2013, Bolin 2014b), is an important background to the formation and experience of generations because the increasingly rapid transformation of our media environments should leave its mark on the experience of each specific generation.

The rest of this chapter will introduce the background to the 'problem of generations'. This will include a review of the previous media research on generations, in which the main analytical concepts relating to generational theory will be presented. A justification for the cross-generational and cross-cultural analysis that is to be made in subsequent chapters will also be given.

The next section will give an introduction to Mannheim's theory and it will describe how it has been developed by others over the years, leading up to the ways in which it has been adopted in media studies and communication theory. This is then followed by a sketch of the empirical research that forms the background to the analysis to follow in subsequent chapters.

Generation theory

Mannheim developed his generational theory as an alternative to Marx's class theory, whereby social class is the historical subject and the driver of social change. To Mannheim, it was rather the generation who was the social subject, but it is also evident that his theory borrowed more than a little from Marx's theory of class. A generation, in Mannheim's sense, is a group of people who have a similar relation to societal events (just as Marx constructed classes depending on group relation to the means of production).

Marx was, however, not the only influence on Mannheim's generation theory. He also picked up the idea from Wilhelm Dilthey about generations as the intermediary between 'the "external" time of the calendar and the "internal" time of our mental lives' (Ricoeur 1985/1990: 111). Thus, Mannheim argued that it was not only age that was significant but also the common generational experiences of people who were born at about the same time and shared similar experiences of the historical process during their formative years of youth. In the focus of this formative moment in youth, Mannheim follows Dilthey, who believed that the formative impressions gained in adolescence provided a 'fund of relatively homogeneous philosophical, social, and cultural guidelines' (Jaeger 1985: 276). By focusing on this formative moment as being decisive for the formation of generations, Mannheim also departs from the more mechanistic ideas of Ortega y Gasset, who points to the repetitive nature of generational exchanges in continuous cycles of equal duration. This 'pulse-rate hypothesis' of generations has had difficulty in gaining ground, although some of the followers of Ortega y Gasset, such as Julián Marías (1961/1970), have carried on the legacy of the Spanish philosopher. Despite some qualifications of Ortega y Gasset's periodisation, for example adjusting the pulse-rate to fifteen years instead of thirty years, Marías had difficulties in providing empirical evidence to back this thesis up (Jaeger 1985).

In theorising the basic structure of generations, Mannheim made a major distinction between generation as 'location' and as 'actuality'. Making analogies with the class position of certain groups in society, Mannheim defined generation as 'the certain "location" (*Lagerung*) certain individuals hold in the economic and power structure of a given society' (Mannheim 1928/1952: 289). The basis for the generational location is naturally year of birth: all people born in the same year, for example, have a 'common location in the historical dimension of the social process' (p. 290).

However, location in time is not enough; it would reduce a generation to an age cohort (cf. Burnett 2010: 48), and thus Mannheim instead introduced the concept of generation as *actuality*. Actuality should be seen as something more than generation as potentiality, and Mannheim develops his concept of generation as actuality against the background of Aristotle's (1997) concept of *entelechy*, a term that in Aristotle refers to the realisation of something that previously existed as potentiality, the 'inner aim' of something. Mannheim picked up the concept of entelechy from German art historian Wilhelm Pinder (1926), who had used it to understand different artistic epochs (Mannheim 1928/1952: 283ff).

Generation as actuality first appears when individuals who occupy the same historical location share the same experiences and are also realised as a generation *for* themselves (as opposed to *in* themselves). These experiences can naturally vary. Some are triggered by dramatic historical-political transformations such as the demise of the Soviet Union and the sudden independent status of countries formerly under Soviet rule (Opermann 2014, Kalmus et al. 2013, Siibak and Tamme 2013). Others might be triggered by media use and cultural experiences, such as cinemagoing (Jernudd 2013) or shared, historically situated music preferences (Sũna 2013). But they all create a certain 'we-sense' (*Wir-Schicht*) among the members of the group (Bude 1997, cf. Corsten 1999).

Furthermore, not everyone who shares the same experience of large and evolving societal events (revolutions, war, famine etc.) will react to these events in exactly the same way. When faced with a specific phenomenon, individuals can 'work up the material of their common experiences in different specific ways', which will result in separate 'generation units' (Mannheim 1928/1952: 304). These generation units can be seen as ways of relating to the same phenomena, and as such make up 'an identity of responses' to the problems at hand (p. 306). Such a compromise includes responses from the social subjects confronted with them. And even if the responses to the events could vary, thus producing generational units that related the historical unfolding in collective − but separate − ways, the role of the event itself was paramount. However, it can be argued that there are also less spectacular, more personal and more mundane, even banal, moments which are formative. Many people can probably recall the moment at which they discovered a cherished artist, film star, or novel that would make a lasting imprint on their lives. For some, it might be Elvis (or Tommy Steele), the Spice Girls or Lady Gaga, for others it might be Marlon Brando, James Dean, Greta Garbo or Marlene Dietrich, and for still others this moment might have occurred when they read *The Catcher in the Rye*, *The Lord of the Rings* or *The Twilight Saga*. These are smaller, much more personal events that might not be as revolutionary in character, but which nonetheless have an individual impact that can be revived and returned to later in life. Of course, there is a collective dimension even to these moments: the rise and popularity of artists and the fan cultures surrounding them indeed occur at a specific point in historical time. But they are *felt* more personally, according to the principle that idols, fan objects and media texts more generally create a specific personal bond between the admirer and the cherished object.

One component in the generational media experience is thus the intimate relationship that develops with media personalities and content from one's formative youth period. This especially concerns music genres and stars. However, people also develop specific, sometimes passionate, relationships with reproduction technologies such as the vinyl record, music cassette tape, comics, and other now dead or near-dead media forms.

Of utmost importance for the formation of such passionate generational experiences is the phenomenon Mannheim calls 'fresh contact', that is, that moment at which an individual is confronted with a novelty of some sort (Mannheim 1928/1952: 293ff). Generational experience is formed through fresh contact, and these experiences are held to impact on all later experience. To Mannheim, the most indelible formative moments were related to historical events, disasters, wars, crises of different sorts, and so on: national traumatic moments such as the murder of the Prime Minister (Olof Palme) or the President (John F. Kennedy), or disasters such as the tsunami on Boxing Day 2006, the Chernobyl disaster in 1986 or its counterpart in Fukushima in 2011, the German invasion of Poland in 1939, as well as more positive historical events such as the end of the Second World War in 1945, the end of the Vietnam war in 1975, the fall of the Berlin Wall in 1989, and so on.

In line with Mannheim's insistence on the importance of fresh contact, it follows that the media technologies and content that one encounters during the formative years of youth can be expected to be the media that will also form all subsequent media experiences (which is why most people, as adults, develop a certain scepticism towards novelties). This is how media generations are thought to develop, with common experiences being connected to specific media technologies or media content (Gumpert & Cathcart 1985). The generation who grew up with the cinema at the birth of the film medium will bring with them this special experience of film as it was phenomenologically perceived at that moment, in that very technological, cultural and social setting. This will bring together persons with similar experiences (and will separate them from those who have not shared these experiences, thus producing generation gaps). This process of bringing together people with the same experiences and shaping their self-perception and 'we-sense' could, in line with Andra Siibak and Nicoletta Vittadini, be called 'generationing': that is, 'the result of the interaction between contextual and fixed traits (such as historical, cultural and social events and experiences) and a cultural process of identity formation developed over time (including narratives, performances and rituals)' (Siibak & Vittadini 2012: 3, see also Siibak et al. 2014).

To Gumpert and Cathcart, such processes of generationing became increasingly relevant for the formation of generations in the twentieth century.

> Prior to the late nineteenth century media explosion, generations came and went, all exposed to and acquiring the same print grammar. Thus media seemed to have little bearing on human time relationships. Though we still think of people as related, or separated in chronological generation time, the rapid advent of new media and the acquisition of new media grammars implies new alignments, shorter and more diverse than those based on generations.
>
> *(Gumpert & Cathcart 1985: 31)*

Gumpert and Cathcart (1985) thus speculated that 'media generations' would be more important than what they called 'chronological generations' (p. 33). They acknowledged that this was not based in any empirical evidence but was an assumption based on the background of historical research that had pointed to the consequences of the invention of handwriting and the development of chirographic cultures (Ong 1967), print (McLuhan 1964) and photography (Sontag 1977). Marshall McLuhan (1964), for example, famously argued via his most famous dictum 'the medium is the message' that the full consequence of the media was that technology (and here he drew more than just a little on the historian of technology, Lewis Mumford [1934/1963, 1967]) was 'altering the desired form of experience', as James Carey (1981: 166) has pointed out.

To Mannheim, 'fresh contact' was a relative concept, and did not only concern 'arriving' phenomena. As individuals come of age, they will encounter many different phenomena that have preceded them. These artefacts might not be 'new' to older people, but to the young person they are; and a young person will approach them from their own vantage point, which in many cases will differ from, for example, the vantage point from which their parents' generation approached them. This is, in fact, one of the main dynamics of change in Mannheim's theory (and thus separates it from perspectives that emphasise functionalist explanation, such as Eisenstadt 1956). Since there is a 'continuous emergence of new participants in the cultural process', there will be a constant flow of 'new age groups', who 'come into contact anew with the accumulated heritage' produced by their predecessors (Mannheim 1928/1952: 293). This is not dissimilar to the historical materialism of Marx when he holds that 'Men make their own history, but they do not make it as they please; they do not make it under self-selected circumstances, but under circumstances existing already, given and transmitted from the past'

(Marx 1852/1995). Mannheim and Marx thus share an interest in explaining historical change, although their main foci for why this happens differ.

Fresh contact is thus always related to previous experience, and for those lacking in experience each fresh contact appears as a novelty. This is also why expressions like 'new media' are relative (if not outright nonsensical), because what is new for one generation is not new for another, older generation. For the very young child all media are new, and it is only as adults that we can distinguish between the new and the old: that is, because we have lived long enough to have seen new media appear in addition to the old media that we were used to. For the toddler, the newspaper and the book are media technologies that are just as new as smartphones and tablet computers. Fresh contact, then, always occurs in a historically specific context in which the encounter between an individual subject and a medium (or its content) takes place.

Indeed, all media have been new at one point in history (Marvin 1988). Today we think of the video as an outdated medium, but there was a time when this was a radically new medium that introduced new ways for viewers to relate to television, for example through timeshifting (Cubitt 1991), but also to film. This was naturally coupled with national variations. In Sweden, with its long-standing tradition of cinema censorship, a wide repertoire of action and horror films with extremely violent representations became accessible. And of course the very young were those who were the early adopters, which was revealed in the fact that families with small children were among the groups in which access was highest (Forsman & Bolin 1997). However, some young people were more active than others; Bolin (1997) analysed a group of young male video enthusiasts from a perspective of generational identity – a group of young men who also converted their consumption into textual production of fanzines and amateur video film-making.

As young people are lacking in experience compared to older people, fresh contacts will have a deeper impact on the young than on the old, and '[a]ll later experiences then tend to receive their meaning from this original set, whether they appear as that set's verification and fulfilment or as its negation and antithesis' (Mannheim 1928/1952: 298). Experience, then, appears in the form of a 'dialectical articulation, which is potentially present whenever we act, think or feel' (p. 298). Furthermore, the individual is most receptive in relation to phenomena that he or she is confronted with around the age of 17 years, give or take a few years, according to Mannheim – who, just like Gary Gumpert and Robert Cathcart (1985), refers to research on the formation of language in an individual, of which it is said that the spoken dialect seldom changes after the age of 25 (Mannheim 1928/1952: 300).

Gumpert and Cathcart argue that how we relate to new and old media is parallel to how we relate to our native language, as opposed to those languages that we might learn later in life. Thus, they stress the tools we have for interpreting the world around us, and the tools we have to aid us when we seek to represent this world for others. In this sense, Gumpert and Cathcart also argue that the media have their own grammar, which needs to be learnt and incorporated. Following

Gumpert and Cathcart, each new medium that an individual is confronted with is read through the grammar of what could be termed our 'native media':

> Even when a person learns several spoken/written languages in a lifetime, the person will generally tend to interact with the world through the bias of the native language. It is our position that the early acquisition of a particular media consciousness continues to shape peoples' world view even though later they acquire literacy in new media. ... For example, those born into the age of radio perceive the world differently from those born into the age of television.
>
> *(Gumpert & Cathcart 1985: 29)*

This means that one might expect a certain homology in, for example, the way that 16- to 22-year-olds relate to a certain media technology and its dominant uses, and that they should bring these relations with them as they grow older.

As Mannheim points to social and cultural factors as important in the formation of the generational experience, his generation theory resembles other theories that have tried to grasp the relation between the individual and society. There are also striking similarities between Mannheim's concept of entelechy – that is, the 'stratified consciousness' and the 'similarity of location' he finds as the common denominator for the generational experience – and Raymond Williams' (1961/1965: 64f) concept of *structure of feeling*: that is, the emotional structure through which we orient ourselves in culture and society. Williams also discusses this in terms of generational succession:

> One generation may train its successor, with reasonable success, in the social character or the general cultural pattern, but the new generation will have its own structure of feeling, which will not appear to have come 'from' anywhere. For here, most distinctly, the changing organization is enacted in the organism: the new generation responds in its own ways to the unique world it is inheriting, taking up many continuities, that can be traced, and reproducing many aspects of the organization, which can be separately described, yet feeling its whole life in certain ways differently, and shaping its creative response into a new structure of feeling.
>
> *(Williams 1961/1965: 65)*

Both the entelechy and the structure of feeling are systems of durable dispositions that guide the apprehensions, actions and practices of the individual, and make him or her orient in society in a way that is naturalised and self-evident to the extent that the individual is seldom fully aware of its mechanisms. These systems will privilege certain ways of acting at the cost of others, although they will never determine individual action in exact and minute detail. Thus, they are open to certain variations in behaviour. Through privileging certain modes of action over others, the concepts of entelechy and structure of feeling are also close to Bourdieu's concept of habitus: that is, the system of durable dispositions that an individual has internalised through family upbringing and education and in relation to the surrounding society, and which imposes on the individual a specific disposition to act. Habitus is 'society inscribed in the body' (Bourdieu 1990: 63) and a 'durably installed generative principle of regulated improvisations' (Bourdieu 1972/1977: 78) that encourages certain ways of acting over others.

Ron Eyerman, June Edmunds and Bryan Turner (Eyerman & Turner 1998, Edmunds & Turner 2002, 2005, Turner 2002) have discussed generational theory in combination with Bourdieu in order to understand 'the conditions under which generations become culturally or politically significant' (Edmunds & Turner 2005: 561). These sociologists draw from Bourdieu the idea that generational struggle over resources is the main component that explains cultural change. Their interest is to explain opposition, protest and resistance, and to complement class as an explanatory concept with generation. This approach has been criticised by sociologists for lacking empirical backup of arguments, for making claims that are too grand and for being too speculative as well as limited in its discussion, with the result that it 'leaves plenty of scope for others' (Jones et al. 2003: 530).

Another criticism that can be made regarding their use of Bourdieu is that they often conflate his concept of generation, which deals mainly with intellectual and artistic generations, along with the broader notion of social generations. The struggle for power that Bourdieu (1983 and 1992/1996) describes among authors and other agents in the literary field in France (or Paris) is indeed one of his most elaborate accounts of field theory and perhaps his finest moment as a field analyst, in parallel to his analysis of the struggles within intellectual generations in the academy (Bourdieu 1984/1990). But the struggle between established artists and newcomers to achieve the most prestigious positions within a literary (or an academic) field is hardly the same as a general struggle between social generations, simply because it is difficult to see generational exchanges as the outcome of struggles. Leaving aside all the problems related to the omission of the rest of Bourdieu's conceptual toolbox for field analysis (e.g., What is the capital struggled over? Which are the consecrating institutions? Who are the other agents of the field?), a struggle presupposes that any agent can actually 'play the game' successfully and win: that is, acquire the more prestigious position within the field. But in what sense could preceding generations 'win' in that sense? Just because there may at times be conflicts between generations over certain values, this does not automatically produce a field in Bourdieu's sense. On this point, Edmunds and Turner are very vague. And although Bourdieu (1990: 95) rightly argues that each field has its own 'specific laws of ageing' (p. 95), these laws are outcomes of the struggle within the field of *other* value forms than age.

So, although Edmunds and Turner use the concept of habitus as an explanation for social action, there is more to say in this discussion, and it is important to emphasise in which way one uses habitus as a concept. A possible way to use generational habitus as a working analytical tool would be to be clear on which social field a certain habitus is activated. Then it could presumably be a point of departure for an analysis of social action, and the concept of habitus would make it possible to study the role of the specific disposition for social action and how a habitus formed in a generational experience as one among several types of experiences. Such an experience would privilege certain approaches to the world based in a generational understanding of it, and, following from that, also makes certain types of actions – as responses to societal happenings – more probable than others. But these actions would occur on a specific field of competition for a certain value (academic, literary, or other value), and not on a field of generations as such. Seen in this way, one could say that the generational consciousness, or identity, provides the generation members with a 'space of possibles' (Bourdieu 1983: 313) in specific fields, in relation to which they can act. The generational experience would then be one, among other experiences, that has been inscribed in the individual agent on a field. This field would be a field of consumption (rather than one of production), where consumers compete for positions in social space with other consumers (Gilleard & Higgs 2007).

Generational experience is, of course, highly dependent on contextual circumstance. Such contextual circumstance is in many ways highly national, not least if we focus on media as an important contributor to experience. And although there might be similarities between national contexts, there are also variations. Sometimes the differences can be quite big, even between neighbouring nation states. Sweden and Estonia, for example, might be bordering countries (although there is the Baltic Sea in-between them), and Tallinn might be the capital that is closest to Stockholm, but their historical backgrounds differ significantly. As generational experience is always rooted somewhere, location in social and geo-political *space* (as well as material *place*) is arguably of importance for the gained generational experience. Dramatic international and even global news events should, for example, mean different things depending on the national vantage point. Such differences make comparative perspectives an attractive method for contrasting national experiences with one another.

Comparative perspectives

If we are to assess the ways in which certain international events are experienced in different national contexts, then we need to adopt comparative perspectives (cf. Deutsch 1987). The advantage of comparative research is that it puts in relief the differences between data, or examples, and through the comparison the specific qualities of each example appear more clearly. Differences, distinctions as well as similarities become visible through comparison. In media studies comparative methods are frequently used to distinguish media systems (Hallin & Mancini 2004, Blumler et al. 1992) or landscapes (Bolin 2003), or to compare media use and audience behaviour (Livingstone & Bovill 2001, Livingstone 2003). Some of this research has exclusively focused on ICTs (e.g. Katz et al. 2003), and some even more specifically on mobile phones (e.g. Campbell 2007, Castells et al. 2007, Bolin 2010, Baron 2010). Sonia Livingstone has, against the background of large-scale comparative projects involving European countries, listed some of the main reasons for doing comparative research, where the aims include:

> improving understanding of one's own country; improving understanding of other countries; testing a theory across diverse settings; examining transnational processes across different contexts; examining the local reception of imported cultural forms; building abstract universally applicable theory; challenging claims to universality; evaluating scope and value of certain phenomena; identifying marginalized cultural forms; improving international understanding; and learning from the policy initiatives of others.
>
> *(Livingstone 2003: 479)*

Comparative research, of course, has its critics. Arguments against comparative research are often grounded in the presupposition that social phenomena are not comparable, as people, countries, cities, and so on, are never exactly the same, and therefore a comparison would be equal to comparing apples with oranges: 'societies and cultures are fundamentally non-comparable and certainly cannot be evaluated against each other', as youth researcher Lynne Chisholm (1995: 22) has argued (cited in Livingstone 1998: 445f). Arguably, however, this depends on what one aims to compare, and for what reason. Quite rightly, one cannot evaluate social phenomena if one's point of departure is a positivist 'dependent/independent variable' approach. However, most qualitative research is posited against such approaches, and if one starts from the assumption that all phenomena actually are fundamentally different, then one does not expect everything to be the same. Such an approach will compare things in order to understand *in which ways* things are different, and on what occasions and in which circumstances – and perhaps also why – some things share similar, or even the same, features.

Most criticisms also focus on the futile project of comparing nations. However, if one is not interested in nations per se, but in the ways that, for example, generations are formed in national (that is, cultural) contexts, or the ways in which generations are distinguished from one another, then many of the arguments from the critics vanish.

When it comes to generational analysis, one obvious comparative aspect is *between different generations*: for example, people with formative experiences made during the Second World War, and those with their formative period during the late 1960s. Presumably, these generations will differ on a number of experiential features, some of which might be related to media and popular culture. Comparing across generational cohorts can shed light on the fresh contact of different generations with the same phenomena. Since Mannheim's argument is that all generations are new participants in a continuous cultural process, one can compare how people who lived with television in the early days of the medium will differ, but also align, with the relations developed by succeeding generations that encounter television at a later stage in the development of the medium. Arguably, there is a big difference between encountering a black-and-white novelty in the late 1950s and encountering the same technology in the era of audio-visual abundance of the early twenty-first century. Not only will the technology of the medium have changed, but so will the surrounding cultural and social context. One could, in fact, discuss whether meeting television as a 17-year-old in 1957 is actually the same thing as encountering the technology as a 17-year-old in 2007.

Another comparative approach is to examine similar generations or cohorts *across different cultural contexts*. If the encounter with a phenomenon at a later stage in the historical process can be instructive for the different ways in which different age cohorts relate to it, and the possible ways in which this can impact on the generational experience, another approach is to look at the phenomenon at the same historical moment but in different national/cultural and social locations. Even if the principles for editing, printing and distributing newspapers are fairly similar across the world, there are vast differences when it comes to how content is organised, in what social and cultural context news is presented, and the conditions under which it is consumed. Such comparisons across national contexts can in fact reveal specificities that one is blind to, if one exclusively looks at one's own cultural context.

Cross-generational and cross-cultural analysis

When it comes to previous research on generations, many studies have focused on specific, single cohorts or generations, for example the 'baby-boomers' of the 1960s (e.g. Wyatt 1993, Jamison & Eyerman 1994, O'Donnell 2010, Björkin 2015). Jennie Bristow (2015), who herself focuses on this generation, argues that this might be because this specific generation was in the early accounts discursively constructed as a generation that made a large impact on society, stood for social renewal and progress, and then later became constructed as a 'problem' in public discourse.

However, not all who have directed their research interest towards generations have focused on single generations. There are several examples of cross-generational studies: for example, Swedish ethnologist Lissie Åström has made cross-generational analyses of female (Åström 1986) and male (Åström 1990) generation chains, focusing on the changes in gender relations over time, and the fostering of class-based femininities and masculinities. Through interviewing family chains in three generations – grandfather, father and son, and grandmother, mother and daughter, respectively – she also captures some of the characteristic gender types of each generation, irrespective of class belonging.

Åström does not use the concept of generation in the same sense as Mannheim and others, but rather emphasises kinship and the succession of family members (cf. Burnett 2010: 24f). As an ethnologist, Åström writes from within an intergenerational relations perspective adopted from anthropology: for example, in Margaret Mead's (1970) famous account of the widening generation gap. However, her main focus is not to study generations but to study the reproduction of masculinity and class.

In a similar vein as Åström, Terhi Rantanen (2005) designed a study on media and globalisation as a case study of four generations in three families in Finland/the UK, China, and Latvia/Israel. Rantanen's objective is not to analyse generations as such, as her interest is in the process of globalisation. One could say that she uses the generation perspective to capture the role of media in social and cultural change, and in this way she seeks to empirically study the processes of globalisation.

Taking their point of departure in the generational theory of Mannheim, Andra Siibak and Virge Tamme analyse three-generation relationships among four Estonian families. Siibak and Tamme discuss the way in which web-based media function as the connecting link between family members of generations, and help in 'establishing and maintaining emotional bonds and enhancing connectedness' (Siibak & Tamme 2013: 84), thus overcoming the increased geographical separation of family members of different generations in late modernity.

Kalmus et al. (2013) have also focused on Estonian generations and media use. Their aim is to analyse intergenerational preference patterns among Estonian media users. They analyse four generations through a national sample and find that the older generations (born 1937–1951 and 1952–1966) are more bound to traditional mass media than are younger generations; whereas Estonians born 1967–1981 make up what Pilcher (1994) calls a 'buffer generation' towards the more digitally oriented younger generations born after 1982, who 'have actively responded to the affordances provided by their "generational location" on the unfolding developmental track of information and communication technologies' (Kalmus et al., 2013: 29).

An analysis of generations centred more specifically on media as technologies (rather than media as content structures) was conducted by myself together with Oscar Westlund (Bolin & Westlund 2009), and focused on the role of mobile phones in shaping Swedish media generations. Taking as our point of departure three specific generational cohorts, we conducted a statistical analysis of user patterns that correlated with general cultural characteristics among mobile owners in an attempt to identify and discuss the character of different generational units in relation to the mobile phone technology. Although the data was longitudinally limited, only spanning five years, it could tentatively be concluded that there was a noticeable consistency in the ways the three cohorts used mobile phones, and that the differences between the three generational groups persisted. The trends identified in this research have been followed up and confirmed in continuous annual surveys by myself, most lately in Bolin (2014a), which will be described in more detail in the sections that follow.

All of the above examples refer to generations analysed in single national settings. However, there are also a few examples of cross-generational *and* cross-national comparisons of generations. Ingrid Volkmer (2006a) has, together with a group of international scholars, conducted a cross-national study on news and public memory, involving nine nations. Volkmer and her team studied how different national media users in three specific generations related, on the one hand, to media technologies and, on the other hand, to international media events or news stories such as the first moon landing, the Second World War, the Vietnam War, the assassination of John F. Kennedy, the Prague Spring, Watergate, Woodstock and so on. The generations studied were born in three cohorts: 1924–1929 (the radio generation), 1954–1959 (the black-and-white TV generation) and 1979–1984 (the Internet generation). It was concluded that these three generations did relate to international media events differently, whereby the oldest were marked by the media being addressed to adults, the middle generation by the growing image culture of television and the youngest by the global and highly individualised, and thus highly differentiated, media flows (Volkmer 2006b: 259). The memories of the oldest, radio generation, were also firmly rooted in the social circumstances in which news was received – the layout of a newspaper page, the fact that one's parents were away at the moment of reception, and so on. The middle television generation, also partly related to social context, but did so in a framework of 'cross-media references', where a news event was learnt of in different media that in combination reinforced the event. The media memories of the youngest 'network generation' did not reveal such social anchorage. Their memories were more fragmented and individual, except for very specific and large-scale media events such as the death of Princess Diana, and integrated into 'an overall entertainment flow' (Volkmer 2006b: 265).

Among the few cross-national or cross-cultural analyses of generations should also be mentioned Piermarco Aroldi and Cristina Ponte's (2012) comparative study of two generations in Italy and Portugal (see also Ponte & Aroldi 2013). Just as was the case in Volkmer's study, Aroldi and Ponte could point to experiential differences due to socio-economic, political and cultural factors. They could show that, although the interviewees were born around the same time during the post-war years (i.e. 1940–1952 and 1953–1965), different national historical events defined the experiences of the respective national generations, where Italian generations were marked by 'the youth movements and protests and the start of terrorism' in the late 1960s, while the Portuguese generations were marked by the Carnation Revolution in 1974, and the end of the Salazar dictatorship.

Thus, one might argue that location in terms of *place* is of equal importance as location in time in the historical process. The specific geo-political and geo-cultural position should have an equal impact on one's experiences as dramatic events should mean different things depending on the spatial position one has. The experience of evolving historical events, like the student revolts in Paris in May 1968, the protests on Tiananmen Square in Beijing or the tearing down of the Berlin Wall, should vary depending on whether one has experienced the event on site or in a mediated form. These are arguably events that have left their mark on people all over the world, but individuals' responses will vary depending on the spatial relationship they have to these occurrences.

Generation and mediatisation

The reason why Mannheim, Ortega y Gasset and others focused on generation in the inter-war years was because they wanted to understand 'the accelerated pace of social change characteristic of our time' (Mannheim 1928/1952: 287). How can one explain that societies actually develop, that new social phenomena arise, and that people think and act differently, producing new social patterns, cultural expressions, and norms and perceptions compared to people of previous times? And, what is it that binds society together during such transformative periods? This 'problem of order', as Dennis Wrong (1994) has summarised it, was the ultimate goal of the sociological thinking at the time (and, of course, always was and still is). By what order is society kept together? What is the relation between the collective whole, and the individual parts?

The question of order versus change is, of course, classical in the social sciences and humanities. It begs for historical, diachronic approaches, with a focus on processes. There are of course several such processual perspectives on social change, but one such approach, which has risen in popularity over the past decade is the perspective of mediatisation. As with all other -isations (globalisation, individualisation, marketisation), mediatisation indicates a temporal development or transformation (cf. Krotz 2007). Furthermore, since there is as yet no agreed perception of the character and scope of the mediatisation process, one should probably talk instead of a variety of mediatisation approaches. In another context I have discussed three such approaches: the institutional, the technological and the constructivist approaches (Bolin 2014c). I will shortly account for these approaches.

The most common of these approaches is by far *the institutional approach*. As one of its main proponents – Stig Hjarvard – argues, this is social theory at the middle range, focusing on the media as institutions, and their relation to other institutions in society (Hjarvard 2013). According to this perspective, the institution of the media – a term which most often indicates the journalistic, news media of the press, radio, television and the Internet – grew increasingly strong over the twentieth century, to the point that their influence on other societal institutions – such as politics, economy, family – became affected. This perspective clearly has its root in the 'media logic' approach of David Altheide and Robert Snow (1979, 1991). The advantage of this perspective is that it is easily operationalised in empirical research. Hence, we have seen a wealth of studies on the mediatisation of politics, corporations, popular culture, war, religion, fashion, storytelling, and so on (see examples of all of these in Lundby 2008, 2009a, 2014). A disadvantage with this institutional approach, as Knut Lundby (2009b) and Nick Couldry (2012: 135f) have pointed out, is that it often brings with it sweeping generalisations, and that one can indeed ask if all media share the same logic, if this logic does not change over time, and if it indeed can capture all the complex dimensions of the social. Another criticism on the processual character of the institutional perspective is that it works with a quite short historical perspective, most often restricting itself to the late nineteenth century (often much shorter). British media sociologists David Deacon and James Stanyer have recently raised this criticism following a review of 93 research articles on mediatisation in 'leading mainstream media and communication journals' between the years 2002–2012. Based on this review they conclude that

> Much mediatization research depends on a presumption rather than a demonstration of historical change, projecting backwards from contemporary case studies rather than carefully designed temporal comparisons.
>
> *(Deacon & Stanyer 2014: 1037)*

While the main proponents for mediatisation theory under attack in this criticism have responded to this argument (Hepp, Hjarvard & Lundby 2015), and the debate continues (Deacon & Stanyer 2015, Lunt & Livingstone 2016), the question of temporal length in the analysis in much mediatisation research remains. There can also be no doubt that longitudinal perspectives are clearly needed.

A third criticism of the institutional perspective on mediatisation is that it works with a quite traditional definition of which media is of influence, and is most often restricted to the traditional mass media press, radio and television (Bolin 2014b). This puts it in contrast to the two other perspectives that both work with longer historical transformations and with wider conceptions of what is meant by 'the media'.

The *technological approach* to mediatisation is not focused on the media as institutions but as technologies. The mediatisation effect is rather at the level of technology and the principles for structuring certain messages above others that technology privileges. If institutional mediatisation has its roots in institutional sociology, then the technological approach is rooted in post-structuralism and anthropology, linguistics and medium theory in the wake of Marshall McLuhan (1964). Jean Baudrillard (1971), for example, argued (also in reference to Walter Benjamin's [1936/1977] account on the fate of art in the age of mechanical reproduction) that media technologies make us engage in simulations of communication. He added that it was specifically their technological capabilities that were the hindrance to full-scale symbolic exchange. The technological approach to mediatisation shares with the institutional perspective a preference for causal explanation. However, whereas the institutional perspective prioritises the media institutions (e.g. journalism) as the cause, the technological perspective points to the codes by which media messages are constructed as the basis of influence. The structuralist element at the root of the technological perspective also gives it a certain deterministic bias that further emphasises technology as the cause of social change.

The *constructionist approach* could be said to integrate both the institutional and the technological perspective, and adds to these a phenomenological dimension of how the media are perceived from within the life-worlds of media users (and producers). This perspective is less objectivist and causal, and deals more with the ways that individual subjects interact with, and sometimes change, the structures within which social action occurs. As institutions and technologies, the media are naturally part of these structures, but the constructionist approach is more inclined to emphasise the interplay between media, individual agency and the formation of structural constraints. Admittedly, the media are privileging certain ways of acting in the world, including the fostering of specific world views before others, but they do not determine these in any all-encompassing way; this is because individual actors, depending on past experiences, will relate differently to 'the media' (as institutions and as technologies) and will also act differently in relation to them.

This perspective also allows for a much more dynamic approach to social change (and stability), is less causal (rather emphasising dynamic interplay), and is much more inclined to think in terms of dialectic dualities, and how media technologies and institutions are always embedded in social contexts. Although these contexts are partly shaped by the media, at the same time they shape the media. Some media technologies can, for example, be appropriated by media users who might then develop usage patterns not anticipated in production. Furthermore, media institutions can produce effects that are neither predicted nor desirable. In each of these cases there will be wider consequences for the social contexts in question. The history of the media is full of such examples: the gramophone was initially thought of as a storage tool for the telephone by its inventor Edison (McLuhan 1964: 264), but later found other uses. Nobody expected the short message service developed for mobile phones to become a success among the general audience (Ling 2004: 214, note 10). Additions to these examples are easy to find in the history of media technologies (Winston 1998).

The constructionist perspective of mediatisation is, however, through its more holistic approach, more difficult to operationalise into delimited empirical analysis. This might also explain why it less often at the forefront of the debate of mediatisation. Given that the media are seen as 'an integral part of fundamental social and cultural processes, and of human life in contemporary (and past) society' (Nowak 1999: 68, my translation), they are also less easy to separate from these complex processes in which they are embedded. This does not mean that the concept is never used by those who encompass this perspective. Swedish communication studies pioneer Kjell Nowak, who was just quoted, was indeed using it already in the 1990s (see, e.g. Nowak 1996: 159ff), inspired by Swedish anthropologist Ulf Hannerz (1990) – also one of the proponents of this specific perspective on mediatisation.

To Nowak (1996: 161f), mediatisation could be seen in at least four ways. The first, and most basic, was the increased dissemination of media technologies and, hence, of an increased spread of media content, in society. We have more media technologies at our disposal, and we have endless opportunities to engage in media content of different sorts and kinds.

The second way in which one could understand mediatisation, according to Nowak, was the impact of the totality of the activities of the mass media in society: their ways of organising and impacting on other social institutions in society (the economy, politics, etc.). This second way of defining mediatisation is similar to that focused on in the institutional perspective that was previously described.

Thirdly, Nowak argued that mediatisation also means that a growing number of things are used as media: that is, as tools for communication in society. We increasingly signal status and group belonging through fashion or style. This is a very visible and profound component of different youth styles, but adults also communicate their status and social belonging through dress codes and stylistic features built around consumer choices. Included in this is that the media in themselves have become tools for such communication, for example when young people distinguish among each other through the type of mobile phone that they have (cf. Vanden Abelee et al., 2014).

Fourthly, and most importantly to Nowak, mediatisation meant that the social interplay between individuals in society is increasingly related to media. Not only do we to an increasing extent connect socially through mobile phones 'and other telemedia' (note that this was written before the advent of smartphones, instant messaging and chat rooms), but

> the media are also a central element in the interplay between people, through the fact that media products and the use of these are often the basis for community, togetherness, and the development of group identities. The media can, furthermore, in different aspects modify and sometimes replace social interaction with other people, and the media can themselves act as participants in, or the object of, social interaction. And in addition, the totality of the system of the mass media can be regarded as a form of social interaction on the societal level.
>
> *(Nowak 1996: 162, my translation)*

Nowak summarised these four types of mediatisation by arguing that social interaction is taking place *within* as well as *with* and *through* 'the media environment'. First, we communicate *within* an increasingly media rich environment where we have access to wider ranging and more differentiated media technologies. Second, these media technologies increasingly allow human–machine interaction, so that we more often communicate *with* technology, for example with Apple's 'intelligent assistant' Siri, who 'understands what you say, knows what you mean, and has the answers you need'.[1] Third, we naturally communicate *through* technologies such as e-mail, SMS and chat rooms, mobile phones, and so on. In Nowak's view, 'the media' should be considered as both a technological structure (a 'material environment') and a symbolic world (a 'mental environment') – both of which are of equal importance.

Nowak was writing in the beginning of the digital restructuring of the media environment, and his examples may sound old (although they are no older than two decades at the time of writing). They are, however, clearly anticipating ideas that are much more common today, such as those proposed in Dutch media theorist Mark Deuze's (2012) *Media Life*. Deuze argues that we have reached a stage in which our whole lives are spent inside the media, similar to how Truman Burbank lived his life in the feature film *The Truman Show* (1998). As Deuze argues, the ending of the film is unsatisfying, possibly naïve, because it is neither possible nor particularly desirable to walk away from the media, as Truman does in the film (Deuze 2012: 254). And indeed, in an age where the media are to us like water to a fish, as Deuze argues, we do not observe them as we go on with our everyday lives; we can only escape the media by making ourselves aware of their presence and consciously avoiding them. But even this is very hard and comes with great costs. Unlike the water, which is the same in all directions, the media are plural, and we do indeed escape some technologies, at least some of the time – we might choose not to have a television set in our summer houses, we turn off the mobile phone at night, we leave the laptop at home when we go on vacation, or we close down our work number on our phone on weekends so that only private friends can call. These are all avoidance strategies that have been reported by media users in interviews, and are signs that we actually go in and out of our water, or at least have the ability to change its character. We can escape some of the media, some of the time, but we would have great difficulties in escaping all of the media, all of the time. Even if we could escape all media technologies, following Nowak and Deuze, the mediatisation process has so fundamentally influenced the ways in which society is constructed, the cultural and social contexts that we share, that this would indeed be no escape at all. Even those who choose to not use Facebook or other social networking sites, for example, will have to live in a world where most other people do, and that fact will not be altered by any individual escape attempt.

Conclusion: a cultural approach to media and generations

Now, one could indeed wonder why so much time has been spent on mediatisation. And, why all these theoretical distinctions? The answer is that the phenomenologically informed approach to mediatisation (what has previously been called the constructionist approach) aligns with the generational perspective of Mannheim, as well as those who have developed the theory of generations since his time. This specific approach to mediatisation shares with Williams, Bourdieu and others a will to transgress the subjectivist–objectivist dichotomy, and should be seen as an attempt at theorising the social as a 'space of possibilities' (Bourdieu 1992/1996) within a framework that is structuring but never determining. This dialectic approach to agency and structure will be adopted in the analysis of generations, and has helped to give structure to the other chapters of this book.

The mediatisation perspective, with its insistence on analysing the role of the media in culture and society as a long-term process, is well in line with such a generational perspective. It can help inform our understanding of how generations are formed in relation to wider social and cultural processes, where the media is one (although not the only) component to take into consideration.

For analytical reasons we might, however, at times need to separate certain concepts and features in our analysis, if only in order to make some components in the analysis stand out more clearly. It is important to see the interconnections between age as a biological factum starting with birth and ending with death, ageing as socio-psychological dimension, and *life course* (including its related features of being in certain life situations, and going through certain specific life-phases such as being a child, a teenager, adult, and senior citizen), and *generation* as a historically specific social formation. Generation is thus 'an age cohort that comes to have social significance by virtue of constituting itself as cultural identity' (Edmunds & Turner, 2002: 7), where 'biographical traits shall coexist alongside historical and cultural characteristics, and where one's belonging to an age group is connected to specific historical experiences, to the development of particular consumption habits' (Aroldi & Ponte 2012: 1).

Such an analysis of the role of generational experience as intersected with age and life-course features means looking at the cultural context as a totality in which experience occurs, since if we do not understand this context, we will not understand the 'responses' that individuals situated in the historical process give. If we believe with Mannheim, and those in his following, that experiences during the formative phase of one's life are of vital importance for which kinds of subsequent action are privileged, then we also need to understand that these habitual features among social groups or formations will also differ along age and life-course parameters. If one has internalised a certain approach to a certain visually based medium (such as television or the smartphone) this internalised approach will be affected if one in later life acquires problems with seeing, to take a drastic example. In that sense age factors, which of course include health features, will affect routinised and habitualised behaviour that has been formed by generational experiences.

Similarly, generationalised behaviour will have to adjust to new situations caused by changes in the life course. One such change happens when one becomes a parent because parenting requires a certain amount of time and energy that cannot be negotiated away, and that comes into conflict with habits connected to one's specific relation to certain media. It does not change the 'media grammars' acquired in relation to particular media habits but it will change everyday engagements with certain media that are less compatible with parenting (extensive and lengthy computer-game sessions, for example). And in the long run, this might also affect the actual relation to the medium in question.

In sum, cultural contextual factors co-vary with age, life phase and generation in a multitude of ways, and to understand the specific nature of these intersecting relations, we need to study them both holistically and longitudinally. In the following chapters I will account for several empirically based examples that can help to formulate a more complex understanding of what role generation plays in the historical process, and how this process in itself is affected and constructed in the interplay between age, life course and generation. However, before we approach this discussion in more detail, we need to elaborate on the analytical model, and more precisely define the conceptual framework for the analysis of media and generations. This is the task of the next chapter.

Note

1 Quoted from http://apple.com/iphone/built-in-apps/, accessed 21 January 2013.

2
AGE, COHORT, LIFE COURSE AND GENERATION

Chapter 1 has briefly introduced the theory of social generations following the work of Mannheim. A few examples of the previous research within this area were given, especially of research that is of relevance for the present argument. It was also argued that generation should be studied in relation to other concepts, such as age and life course. It also described why process-oriented and holistic perspectives are important if we are to understand the role that generational experience plays in the wider historical process. In addition, the merits of comparative perspectives were outlined, and it was explained how cross-cultural and cross-generational approaches could be vital for a cultural understanding of media and generations.

However, as the concept of generation is often used in popular and semi-academic accounts, there is a need to more exactly clarify the relationship between age, life course (and related concepts such as life situation and life phase) and generation, since these are different dimensions that all have a bearing on the ways in which we might think, and indeed perceive of, social and cultural change. Age, life course and generation are concepts that are also used in everyday parlance and, as Pierre Bourdieu has pointed out, one of the main difficulties for the social and cultural analyst is to break with the spontaneous sociological observations that one makes in everyday life and avoid reducing 'the social world to the representations that agents have of it' (Bourdieu 1989: 15). While a neurophysicist or a biomedical researcher work within the framework of a specialised language that few outside of their field are capable of understanding, most social and cultural scholars work with concepts that are also used by lay persons and have meaning outside of the academy.

Thus, the concept of generation is widely used, and in buzz discourse concepts such as 'net generation' (Tapscott 1998), 'digital natives' (Prensky 2001), 'generation X' (Coupland 1991) and 'generation me' (Twenge 2006) are flourishing. We are also equipped with more academic reflections on the 'global generation' (Edmunds & Turner 2005), the 'digital generation' (Buckingham & Willett 2006, Taipale 2016) and even the 'social media generation' (Huang 2014), without necessarily having these defined in any precise manner in relation to other parameters related to ageing and the various situations individuals confront during their lives (cf. Aroldi & Colombo 2013, Fortunati 2011).

In Chapter 2 we will concentrate the discussion more clearly on the theoretical and conceptual framing of the generation problem and especially the relation between social generation, age, birth cohorts, life situation, life course and related features. This chapter will start with an account of the respective conceptual areas and their previous usage in research, and the second half will discuss the ways in which they might relate and have a bearing on one another. This will thus make up the theoretical model that the subsequent chapters will rely on.

Age and memory

Age is among one of the basic background variables in general sociological analysis, and it has also been at the centre for media audience analysis, especially within the more administratively oriented audience research. As a biologically founded, rather than socially formed, feature, age is inexorable in its constant adding of years to years. This, however, means that age is a condition that is not stable but always in flux: you are only 18 for one year of your life, and you cannot return to that age.

Of course, a common way for people to explain away the fact that they are ageing is that you might have reached a certain age biologically, but you are young in spirit. And some people return from a health check happily announcing that the doctor had said that they were as healthy as a 17-year-old. And of course, you might distinguish between your biological age and your mental perception of how old you are, and you can naturally be in different physical shapes over the course of your life. Some will even go through surgery to try to appear younger than their biological age, but you cannot change the fact that you are born at a certain date in a certain year, and that the distance to that date is increasing every day.

As biological age increases, certain societal privileges and restrictions follow: you are not allowed to take a driver's licence before a certain age (18 in Sweden), your access to tobacco and alcohol is restricted by law to certain ages, in the labour market you are not allowed to work below a certain age, and there are restrictions on the age at which you can take a loan at a bank. All of these things are related to your age as defined by what year you were born, and it will not matter if you claim that you feel like 55 when you have reached the age of compulsory retirement at 67 (in Sweden), or that at the age of 18 you are more mature than most 22-year-olds, when you are stopped from buying a bottle of wine at Systembolaget, the monopoly for alcoholic beverages in Sweden, because the age limit is set to 20 years.

In contrast to your age, which you will constantly abandon over the course of your life in the sense that each year you become one year older, it is very hard to leave your generation. Whether you want it or not, the biographic and demographic fact that you were born in a certain year makes you predestined to encounter many things in life at the same time as your coevals. You will all enter school together, you will go through a series of routines that all kids in a certain society will go through, take the same immunisations for child diseases, go to the school dentist, you will be able to vote for the first time simultaneously, you will retire around the same time, and so on. One might think that if all children encounter these things, they will develop common experiences. However, even within a specific national setting, although all people go to the dentist at the age of five for the first time, the practice of dentistry still changes over time, and so the farther away from another individual you are born, the more different the experience will be.

When it comes to media use, age is and has always been of concern to parents, teachers and other socialisation agents. There are various classification schemes at which age children are fit to watch certain television programmes, or cinema films. Children's games (digital or analogue) often come with recommendations for which age they are suited. If you enter a bookshop to find out what book you want to buy for your children, you ask the staff for a book suitable for children this or that age, and so on.

In media research, whether it is academic, critical research, or industry-led administrative audience research, age is one of the most common background variables for statistical analysis, together with other socio-demographic and socio-economic parameters. The most common way to account for the age patterns of media use is to cluster age groups together, looking for commonalities or breaking points in behaviour. In administrative research within the media and culture industries, this is of course natural, since specific age groups are what advertisers by tradition want to reach. Age is thus one of the most important ingredients in the construction of the audience commodity, as packaged and sold by the media and culture industries to advertisers (Bjur 2009). The systems of measurement used for constructing the audience commodity have changed over the years, and algorithmically based constructions of media user behaviour are succeeding the old, demographics-based models for the audience commodity; however, there are tenacious structures that make, for example, advertisers and others who want to 'buy audiences' prefer the traditional sociological variables of age (education, sex, and socio-economic status) before the algorithmically produced behavioural patterns of the 'digital consumer' (Bolin & Andersson Schwarz 2015). So, even if age in the digital world is a less efficient analytical tool for optimising the audience commodity, tradition and habit privilege older marketing practices.

Aside from those perspectives that focus on age as a parameter in sociologically informed audience analysis, there is also a huge body of research on age as related to ageing and the features involved in the process of becoming old. Much of this research is of little relevance for the analysis of generation formation, but that part which deals with memory studies is pertinent. On the one hand, the field of memory studies is important for methodological and analytical reasons, as we need to understand something about how memory works in order to be able to evaluate how experience, including media experience, is articulated in interviews and other types of empiric materials. If we, for example, want to understand the specific experience of growing up and coming of age several decades ago, then we must ask people in interviews, or read autobiographic material that accounts for those times. These accounts need to be evaluated in the analysis, and the quality of our analysis will depend on how we understand the workings of a person's memory, and what triggers the act of remembering.

On the other hand, and more specifically, memory studies are important for the understanding of how nostalgic memories are triggered and formed. Nostalgia, being a specific sentiment directed towards the past, deals less with 'how things actually were' and more with the inner landscape that is accounted for, and how lack, loss and longing, which are important parameters in the nostalgic imagination, are constituted in the minds of those belonging to a specific generation (Keightley & Pickering 2012).

There are, however, several traditions within memory studies, which all have different ontological and, above all, epistemological approaches to memory. Broadly, one could distinguish between three types of approaches in memory studies: psychological, sociological and cultural. The lines between these are not clear-cut and there are significant overlaps, but if one, for the sake of clarity, should give a somewhat generalised and reductive account, one could say that *psychological* studies of memory concentrate on individual memory formation from a cognitive-psychological perspective, whereas *sociological* approaches emphasise the collective and social nature of memory formation. Methodologically, however, they are often similar, building on controlled surveys, and experiments, and using hypothetico-deductive approaches (see e.g. Schuman & Corning 2014). *Cultural* perspectives to memory studies could be said to ask similar questions as do sociologists, but have more interpretative approaches to understanding memory. Empirical focus in cultural memory studies can thus also be literary texts, monuments, and other cultural or mediated expressions picked from, journalism, advertising, cinema, television and music, for example. As Ruth Teer-Tomaselli has pointed out in reference to Halbwachs's work, there is not necessarily a contradiction between the two perspectives, but instead 'studying the same objects' takes place from different ontological and epistemological positions (Teer-Tomaselli 2006: 227). As will be shown in the analysis of nostalgia, there are insights to be drawn from the more positivist psychological accounts of memory formation, despite the different scientific-philosophical points of departure.

It is, of course, common wisdom that memory is selective. However, in terms of how memory affects the generationing process, it is important to know just how this selection process occurs. This is not so much a question of judging the accuracy of memories, gauged in relation to some perceived reality, but is more about understanding how experience is formed as such, including how and why 'imagined' or 'prosthetic memories' (Landsberg 1995) are formed. Alison Landsberg describes prosthetic memories as 'memories which do not come from a person's lived experience in any strict sense' (Landsberg 1995: 175), with theoretical inspiration from Baudrillard's (1983) theory on simulation and simulacra, that is, the idea that that we live in a world of copies without origins. However, it seems to me as if Landsberg makes too sharp a distinction between mediated experience and 'lived experience', and one can well wonder why mediated experiences of events, for example news events from distant places, are not real. Is it not rather another type of experience: one that is no less real, but experienced by other means and from other times and places? Her analogy with prosthetic arms would suggest this. A prosthetic arm may not be the arm that a person was born with, but it would still be an arm, albeit another sort of arm, acquired at a later point in life than birth. But it would still work as an arm, and the actions that the person carries out with it would have real-life consequences. Memory is the same, and one of the main focuses of culturally oriented memory research is to understand *how* something has been selected and incorporated in a person's memory, especially when it comes to nostalgic memories.

It has also been pointed out that memories are the outcome of the process of remembering. The process of remembering 'appear[s] to shape and frame cognitive activity that originated from experiences', and means that 'our memories become more and more virtual in the course of time: elaborated elaborations of elaborations' (Kumar et al. 2006: 213). So, rather than being an account of what objectively happened, memory is a narrative that is successively worked on by the individual and is refined each time it is returned to. Furthermore, this means that there is a collective dimension to memory where people's accounts of memories are narrated in a social environment and thus sometimes adjusted to fit that environment (Halbwachs 1950/1980). Furthermore, this environment is not only social but is also mediated, and input into these narratives does not only come from other individuals but also comes from the media, which 'offer behavioural, auditory, and visual concepts; verbal, graphical, and pictorial instruments to designate, symbolize, or represent experienced and/or mediated events' (Kumar et al. 2006: 213).

Cohorts

Age cohorts, or birth cohorts can be described as 'those persons born in the same time interval and ageing together' (Ryder 1965: 844). This is a very descriptive definition; some would also add the potential that comes from being born together at a specific historical point in time. Thus, June Edmunds and Bryan Turner add to this definition that a cohort is 'a collection of people who are born at the same time and thus share the same opportunities that are available at a given point in history' (Edmunds & Turner 2002: ix). Birth cohorts, then, can be anticipated to share some defining characteristics, for example a certain kind of behaviour in media consumption, a common habit and world view developed among coevals (that is, people of the same age). Quite often the concept of generation is used interchangeably with age cohort, especially in everyday parlance, such as when we talk of 'thirty-somethings', 'the young generation', the '1970s generation', and so on. In some academic research, generation is also used to describe birth cohorts, and one can indeed find scholarly work discussing generations in this way without referring even once to generation theory (e.g. Gunther et al. 2009). And for sure, there are some parts of this usage where generational traits (experiences, for example) are alluded to, but most often this is a type of everyday parlance that requires less precision, and where contextual factors in the speech situation will determine the meaning of the usage. A common example and point of confusion is when people talk of the 1960s generation. By this, some will mean 'people born during the years 1960 to 1969', which would be an age cohort (e.g. Björkin 2015), while others would refer to 'people who were active in student protests, movements or taking part in the 1960s popular music scene more generally', which would be a usage more in line with generational theory. Some of this research expands on Mannheim's concept of generation to also include those who did not actively take part in, for example, protest movements (e.g. against the Vietnam war) but who were affected in a mediated way by the media attention given to this group of activists, which had consequences for the wider society and hence became formative for less culturally or politically involved citizens of those societies (e.g. Eyerman 2002: 62).

The people of the generation active in the protest movements in the late 1960s are most often referred to as the 'baby boomers', especially when discussed in the contexts of Britain and the US. The most significant trait of this birth cohort is that it is large − 'the sheer number of "boomers" dwarfs those born either side of it', as Gilleard and Higgs (2007: 20) describe it. In that sense they make up a demographically interesting category because exceptionally large cohorts pose some logistical societal problems, such as the demand for larger cadres of teachers at certain moments, high pressure on the labour market when the cohort reaches the age of entering into the job market, and, maybe most pressing for many Western countries, a strategy for handling the situation when an exceptionally large cohort reaches the point of retirement.

However, it should be noted that the demographic category of baby boomers 'has more meaning for North Americans than it has for Europeans' (Gilleard & Higgs 2007: 20), as Europe was a continent where the increase in births was more modest (e.g. in Finland), where birth rates had stagnated or were in decline (as in Eastern Europe), or where the increases did not match those in the US at that time (as in France and the UK) (Gilleard & Higgs 2007: 22). As Jennie Bristow (2015: 9) shows, there were in fact two distinct 'booms' in the British birth rates: one immediately after the Second World War, and another in the years around 1960. Similar differences in relation to the US baby boom extend to most parts of the world.

The reason why many generational studies have focussed on the baby boomers, argue Chris Gilleard and Paul Higgs (2007), is that this birth cohort was the first cohort to be formed in relation to the consumer market, giving rise to a 'generational field' (in Bourdieu's sense) where 'the underlying logic is structured by consumption, a post-scarcity consumption that supports the search for distinction' (Gilleard & Higgs 2007: 25). This is in line with analyses of the rise of post-war youth cultures (Fornäs & Bolin 1994), with the development of youth cinema in the United States in the 1950s (Doherty 1988), or the way that media users develop strategies of distinction through excessive consumption practices and elaborate preference patterns for popular culture material (Bolin 1994). However, the fact that large cohorts become of interest to the consumer market and advertising does not automatically provoke the development of a generational consciousness, irrespective of the fact that consumer patterns might be a common denominator. This is the point where there have been conflations of age cohorts and generations.

Such conflations are in fact rather common. In a widely cited work such as Zukin et al.'s (2006) study on political participation, the generational typology is constructed of people born pre-1945 ('the dutifuls'), 1946–1964 ('the baby boomers'), 1965–1976 ('Generation X') and 1977 and after ('the dotnets'). To be fair, the authors are cautious enough to describe these as 'potential generations', and also warn that 'drawing boundaries between generations is a risky business' (Zukin et al. 2006: 17). For the most part, they use the concept of cohort rather than generation in their study. However, despite these precautions, surprisingly many have adopted their categorisation uncritically. The problem with such typologies is that the concept of generation becomes conflated with the concept of age and age cohort, and that these groups cannot be said to make up a self-perceived generation in the same sense as that in which Mannheim theorises the concept, and the way in which it has been used in sociology since the 1920s. If we take seriously the distinction between generation as locality and actuality introduced by Mannheim then it is hard to imagine that someone born in 1946 would be affected in the same way by the same societal event as someone born in 1964, even if we restrict the analysis to the same geo-cultural space. And if perceptions differ, then there will be no shared experience that could be the basis for a self-perceived generational identity that would make up a realised generation. For one, such a broad categorisation sidesteps the idea of formative years because these do not occur at the same time. Zukin et al.'s study is based in political science, and even if it would be applicable there, it is very hard to see how media experiences during the mid-1970s could have the same formative influence on someone who is in his or her mid-thirties as they would have on a 15-year-old. Or, to pick a popular culture example: the impact of the Beatles on a 20-year-old will probably differ from that of a three-year-old child. And the effect of listening to Elvis in the late 1950s would have differed from the effect of listening to the same record in the late 1970s, when Elvis was no longer alive, and when the image of an overweight and drug-abusing Elvis was hard to forget while listening.

Furthermore, Zukin et al.'s (2006) study of 'generational groups' builds on a construction of age cohorts in the United States. This means that the social subjects, that is, the generation cohorts constructed by the researchers, are explicitly constructed on the basis of a North American context (Zukin et al. 2006: 17ff), which does not necessarily correspond to other cultural, political and social settings. So, even if one would accept the generational typology that they constructed (and as is probably clear from my account here, I hesitate in doing this), it does not follow that these are applicable in, for example, Swedish, Spanish, Greek or other European settings, and maybe even less so in South American, Asian or African social, political and cultural environments (c.f. Gilleard & Higgs 2007: 20). Again, this is not so much the fault of Zukin et al., since they do not argue for a global applicability of their results, but rather of those who have uncritically adopted their generation cohorts.

Thus, one needs to distinguish clearly between age (and age cohorts), life course and generation (cf. Burnett 2010: 41ff). Cohort is the statistical unit used in positivist inquiry, in which its fixed boundaries are identified and objectified by the researcher. In Mannheim's words, a cohort is a generation as locality: it has its position in the historical process fixed by the fact that it is constructed of people born in the same years. But it differs from generation as actuality in that an age cohort is 'devoid of sociological content' (Närvänen & Näsman 2004: 73).

Most generation analyses that follow Zukin et al.'s periodisation principles also define generations that are divided by sharp breaking points at a specific year (which in the most reflexive accounts are also justified and argued for). The most basic generation cohorts build on a decade structure where people born during specific decades are labelled: the 1960s generation, for example. This kind of labelling is problematic for several reasons, as has rightly been pointed out in previous scholarly debate (e.g. Jaeger 1985, Spitzer 1973). First, because the continuous flow of births makes any attempt at drawing sharp lines between generations problematic. Second, because it can refer to those born during this decade, just as well as to those who had their formative years in this decade (and hence were mainly born in the 1940s). Third, because there is a vast difference between those who had their formative years in the beginning of the decade, compared to those born during the student revolts and the flower power movement (O'Donnell 2010, Jamison & Eyerman 1994).

Zukin et al. (2006) rightly describe their objects of analysis as 'potential generations', since they are based on age cohorts. Such a potential generation would correspond to generation as locality in the terminology of Mannheim. Potential generations are most often constructed as successive cohorts, one following upon another, just as Zukin et al. have constructed them. A problem with this is that the lines between generations are sharp, and one can wonder to what extent it is meaningful to distinguish between someone born in 1964 and 1965. Why, for example, would someone coming of age and having their formative years around 1980 differ from someone having his or her formative period one year later? And could one not suspect that those born in 1964 would have more in common in terms of experience, cultural taste, etc., with someone born in 1965 than with someone born in 1946?

For those reasons it might be better to construct more narrowly defined cohorts that do not directly follow on from each other but have been extracted from a smaller age range in order to make it more likely that they would also share the same or at least similar experiences. In this way one could argue that the likelihood of this potential generation actually being realised as a self-perceived group would increase. The ways in which one chooses the specific age cohorts are of course of utmost importance here. The more that they are constructed in relation to specific historic contexts (just as Zukin et al. do), including the context of the media landscape and the rise of new media forms or genres, the more the potentiality of there actually being a realised generation increases.

The potential generations shown in Figure 2.1 were constructed on the basis that the age cohorts had their formative years in different media contexts: for the generation of the early 1930s, having their formative years shortly after the Second World War, radio and the press are dominant media, and to a certain extent cinema, while for those born in the early 1950s the arrival and establishment of television

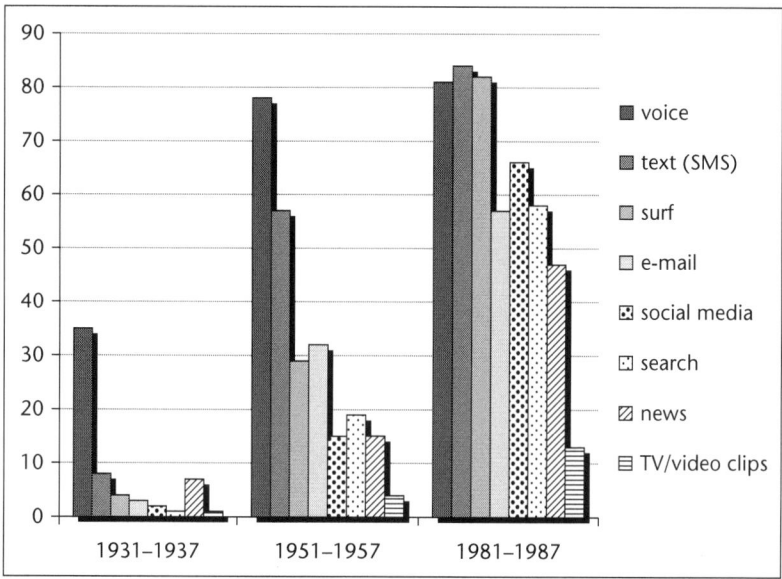

FIGURE 2.1 Daily use of different mobile functions among three age cohorts of Swedish mobile owners

Source: National SOM Institute survey for the year 2013. Data collected Q4 2013.

in the 1960s, the LP record and tape recorders were expected to have an impact. The respondents born in the early 1980s had their formative years at the time when mobile phones, computer games and personal digital media were introduced and established in Sweden, and when television changed from a public service monopoly to a plural television landscape of both commercial and public service media.

However, even if the potentiality of the realisation of the respective generations increases, we cannot know this from pure statistical analysis alone. Even if we can conclude that the respondents born in the early 1980s seem to have naturalised a broad range of communication functions on the mobile compared especially to the early 1930s generation, but also to those born in the early 1950s, this says nothing about how the respective groups view themselves in terms of generation or generation unit, or what meanings they ascribe to their use. In order to judge to what extent the generation is realised, we would need to either make a more fine-tuned statistical analysis – based in other types of questions than pure access or frequency of use, for example questions regarding attitudes towards media use – or we would have to change the methodology altogether, for example turning to interviews, where questions of self-perception and attitudes can be more deeply penetrated.

A generation, in contrast with an age cohort, irrespective of how the cohort is constructed, also needs to perceive of itself as a generation to fulfil Mannheim's idea of generation as actuality. *Life course* or life cycle analysis, on the other hand, concentrates on the individual and his or her trajectory through history.

Life course

Life-course analysis deals with 'the social and historical changes that impact a particular generation at a particular point in time', and is 'shaped by both internal psychological and external sociological processes' (Harrington & Bielby 2010: 430). Psychological understandings of the life course often emphasise hierarchical developments among individuals in, for example, moral orders (Erikson 1959), and often take the form of a 'narrativized … journey of the self' (Burnett 2010: 43). In its sociological understanding, it 'refers to the age-structured sequence of roles, opportunities and experiences that an individual moves in and out of, and that are influenced by macro-structural forces as well as human agency' (Harrington & Bielby 2010: 446).

It is naturally evident that all such narratives do not follow the same trajectory, but there are at the same time general phenomena that each individual in a given society is confronted with: kindergarten, school, working life, and so on. There are also some phases of life that are common for many – although not all – people, for example having children, going to school, marrying, and so on. This means that many people (but not everyone) will share the experience of marriage and child-rearing, which will contribute to a shared experience that can make up common combinations as a basis for specific generational units. Sociological perspectives thus focus on life course as 'general patterns of stability and transition' (Harrington & Bielby 2010: 430), such as those related to childhood, youth, adulthood and late life. In sociologically informed youths studies, for example, youth is seen as a *life phase* that is marked by certain features (cf. Närvänen & Näsman 2004). To be young is to face certain societal hopes and fears about what youths are, what they will become, and how this will impact on society in the future. These expectations in terms of hopes and fears will have a bearing on how you will relate to others and to societal development in general (Bolin 2004).

Life phases or life stages, as many use the terms interchangeably (and I will join that group), are not stable categories over time. As US historian John Gillis (1974: 2f) has shown, youth as a separate life stage between childhood and adulthood developed successively from the mid-eighteenth century in preindustrial society and gradually developed and expanded to the present age. This fact has been thoroughly researched and debated within historically oriented youth cultural research, especially in Europe (Mitterauer 1986/1991). Much of this research is in fact based in the changing premises for this life phase and its rapid prolongation after the Second World War, when youth became an important consumption category for the culture and media industries (Bolin 2004, cf. Hebdige 1988).

Youth as a life phase can also be analysed from biological, psychological, social and cultural perspectives. However, although some of these perspectives might seem more universal and stable than others, even the category of biological youth varies over time and space. As Austrian youth historian Michael Mitterauer has shown, puberty and sexual maturity, which are markers of the transition to biological youth, have decreased in age over the past couple of hundred years in

Europe. There are also geographical differences along the north–south axis, where the moment of sexual maturity arrives earlier in the south compared with the north of Europe (Mitterauer 1986/1991: 12ff). Also socially, the youth life phase has changed historically. Youth research has long since pointed to the changed living conditions for the young, the prolongation of youth through the increased length of schooling, postponed entry into the labour market, and the consequences this has had on the experience of being young (cf. Fornäs & Bolin 1994). Again, it needs to be stressed that historically these conditions have been different depending on which geo-cultural area is in focus, at what specific point in history and in what social class context the youth years have been spent (Mitterauer 1986/1991).

There are also certain circumstances that are common during the life course, and which are defining for different life phases. We can call these circumstantial moments for *life situations*. Being employed, having children, being a student, and so on, will affect the amount of time it is possible to spend with the media, as well as which media are accessible and on what occasions. Children and pensioners, for example, have more free time to spend on media consumption than do those who work (Gahlin 1977). So, individuals enter into certain phases of life, encountering certain kinds of situations common to many, but not all, others within this same life phase. Not all people reach retirement, for example, and the duration of different situations can vary substantially; that is, we can be within certain phases or situations of life during our life course for different durations of time. Some people might marry and divorce within the temporal framework of a year, which means that this specific phase of life is comparatively short. Others might marry at an early age and stay within marriage for the balance of their lives, celebrating 50, 60 or even 70 years of marriage.

Life phase and life stage are thus tightly connected to age as a linear category, and as a phase of life that you enter into, but that you also at one point in time or another leave (ultimately through death). The situations that we face in different life phases will impact on our generational experience. As there are ways of life that are dominant in any culture, we will share many of these experiences with many, although not all, other people born around the same time. However, it is also important to note that certain life phases, for example childhood, mean different things in different historical contexts (Hareven 1982). This is obvious if we consider life phases in the context of media use and the media landscape that surrounds each generation. Having one's childhood in the early 1900s meant that one spent one's days in a much less media-saturated environment than those who spent their childhood in the early 2000s. Whether this means anything for the generational experience is naturally an empirical question. One is tempted to think that it is not entirely improbable that the media environment, in conjunction with the general view on children in society, the expectations from schools and other institutions that the child is confronted with, as well as the socially expected parent-child relationships, will have an impact on the experience of childhood as a phase in life. But only empirical research can establish if this is a fact or not.

Quite naturally, there is no denying that children and young people (and adults as well) indeed have changed behaviours, preferences, habits, and so on, due to the introduction of new media (and new technologies more generally). However, it is important to distinguish between which types of media user patterns in preferences and behaviour can be attributed to life phase and which can be attributed to generation. Some types of media behaviour will be more likely when people seek to adjust themselves to a specific life situation, in a specific phase of life, while other kinds of media behaviour will be related to generational cohort.

Life situations, as the specific social circumstances you find yourself in over the duration of the life course, are, contrary to age, not necessarily linear. There are certain life situations that you can enter into, in order to then leave, and, at a later point in the course of your life, re-enter. Some people go in and out of marriage, for example, and following from that you can also go in and out of being a parent for small children in order to then re-enter into that life situation at a later point in life. If this happens, this life situation will not be exactly the same as the first time you were in it because you will bring with you the previous experience, but it will be structurally similar in many ways. One can only be a first-time parent once in a lifetime, and all later children will be born into a social situation that is somewhat unique to them as individuals. Take again the photo from the cover of this book. My great-grandmother Karin gave birth to thirteen children. The first was born in 1896, and her youngest child Sven was born 1922, making him 26 years younger than his oldest sister Agnes. In terms of family succession, all of Karin's children were second generation to her, but they were born at different points in historical calendar time, and into very different historical contexts. Not only had there been a world war between the births of Agnes and Sven but a range of other social facts had also changed: women had been allowed to vote in national elections, new media such as radio were introduced, Norway was no longer a part of Sweden, and the spelling reform of 1905 lay between them. So, even if Agnes and Sven were *contemporaries* of the same kinship generation (that is, being alive at the same time), they did not share generational belonging as *coevals* (being of the same age) (see Eyerman & Turner 1998: 93 for a discussion of contemporaries and coevals). In fact, my grandmother and many of the oldest siblings had not lived at home for a very long time, and some of them, including my grandmother, had moved from the northern parts of Sweden to Stockholm, 650 kilometres south of the family home.

Analytical approaches to age, life course and generation

Life course, life phase, age and life situation are thus relevant parameters in sociological analysis, including audience and media-use analysis, which is clearly illustrated in Signe Opermann's (2014) study of generational news media use in Estonia. Opermann's study built on quantitative survey data from 2002 through 2011, and reveals how certain patterns of news-topic preferences are stable for each cohort over time, while others vary.

Table 2.1 can be discussed from both an age perspective, as well as from generational and life phase perspectives. In the table, rankings 1–5 have been highlighted to reveal patterns over time and between cohorts. Not surprisingly, the youngest cohort is the one that changes the most over the decade. None of the preferences are ranked in the same way over the years, which can be explained by the fact that young people, in accordance with youth cultural theory (Bolin 2004), have not yet achieved a stable identity of their own, and hence no stable patterns of preference, but are rather trying out different options and identity positions. This is one age-related, basically socio-psychological explanation for the variation over the years.

The most stable categories of preferences of media topics for the youngest cohort are 'education, learning' and 'youth life', which might not be so surprising since the respondents are still in school and are still to be considered 'youth' even by the end of the period.

Another age-related feature to note is that interest in healthcare issues are highest and most stable over the years among the two oldest cohorts, possibly because of age factors, since age-related health conditions can be expected to increase with growing age. This is contrary to the figures on the youngest cohort, where respondents were between 15 and 25 years at the time of data collection. This could be explained in terms of an age-related effect, on the assumption that young people have fewer problems with their health and accordingly less interest in looking for information on health matters. The youngest cohort's preference for questions on 'youth life' and 'education and learning' is consistent with youth cultural studies, where it is noted that young people are interested in the lives and activities of other young people. Since young people for the most part are also still in school, they also – presumably – have an interest in questions concerning education: that is, an interest triggered by the conditions of this specific phase in life.

As opposed to the youngest cohort, the oldest cohort is the most consistent in their preferences. Their taste patterns are long since established and media use has evolved into an everyday routine. The next to oldest cohort also reveals a very stable preference pattern over the years, with a clear consistency when it comes to the three most preferred areas of interest.

Some features, such as the interest in television, are similar across all respondents: for example the interest in national news, which all but the youngest generational cohort have the greatest preference for, except at the time of the first data collection, when this group was only 15 years old. Six years later, at the age of 21, the respondents in this generational cohort show more appreciation of national, local and foreign news, which suggests that we are facing an *age effect*, where interest in news appears to increase after the teenage years have passed.

If the 'children of freedom' and the 'transition' generation cohorts can be assumed to still be in education (more so the younger cohort, of course), then the 'space race' generation, as parents to the children of freedom, also should have an interest in education. It is thus indicative that the two older generations have less interest in

TABLE 2.1 Ranked preferences for news topics among five generational cohorts of Estonian media users 2002, 2008 and 2011. The table is an edited version of Opermann (2014:128f)

Topic	The post-war generation (b. 1932–1941)			The early Soviet time generation (b. 1942–1957)			The space race generation (b. 1958–1971)			The transition generation (b. 1972–1986)			The children of freedom (b. 1986–1997)		
	2002	2008	2011	2002	2008	2011	2002	2008	2011	2002	2008	2011	2002	2008	2011
Estonian news	1	1	1	1	1	1	1	1	1	1	1	1	5	1	1
Local news	2	2	2	2	2	2	2	2	2	2	2	2	9	3	3
Health care	3	3	3	3	3	3	5	3	4	7	11	8	12	15	14
Social problems, social security	4	4	4	7	5	7	11	7	6	16	5	12	23	17	18
TV programmes, films	6	6	5	5	9	5	3	9	6	3	6	7	2	7	6
Foreign news	10	5	6	4	7	4	6	6	3	8	3	3	7	7	2
Current affairs, opinions	9	7	7	12	8	6	14	10	5	20	10	9	22	14	16
Humour	14	10	8	11	6	8	9	5	7	6	4	5	1	4	7
Nature, environment	5	9	9	8	13	10	12	17	13	15	27	23	16	28	27
Crime, police, law	7	8	12	10	4	9	8	4	11	4	7	10	10	8	10
Home, family, children	11	14	16	9	12	13	4	8	9	10	7	4	13	16	25
Education, learning	19	26	18	15	21	16	10	13	12	5	12	6	3	5	4
Music	–	24	29	–	31	30	–	29	27	–	23	22	–	9	8
Youth life	26	33	32	20	34	32	16	22	25	9	15	15	4	2	5

Comment: The question was formulated as: 'What fields or media topics are you interested in? Mark all topics you would be most likely to follow'. The answers were then ranked for each generational cohort. The item 'music' was not included in 2002. The cohorts were constructed on the basis of societal developments in Estonia, including changes in media system and technology. For a more elaborate account of the generational groupings, see Opermann (2014:89ff).

this topic, which demonstrates an effect of the specific *life phase* that these three cohorts are in. Life phase factors are most probably also behind the fact that the young seem to have little interest in health issues, in contrast to the older cohorts.

When it comes to speculations about the *generational effects*, ten years is of course too short a time to establish any firm evidence or even strong indications. However, there are results that also point in this direction. If we return to the oldest cohorts, we could conclude that their patterns of preferences were the same over the studied years. On the basis of this, we could explain this consistency with the fact that the respondents in this group, being between 60 and 70 years in 2002, and between 70 and 80 years in 2012, had acquired a firm and established identity, including preferences for types of information. However, we can see that this stability also produces a generational preference pattern, which follows the respondents over the years. We could, therefore, discuss the possibility of there being a generational effect, where respondents born around the same time have developed similar taste patterns.

The dynamic interplay between age, cohort, life course and generation

On a general level of analysis, the stages in the life course tend to privilege people to be situated in specific life situations that are common to many, although not all, individuals in society. There are certain practices that people engage in while they are young and go to school, and there are certain preferences and tastes that accompany these practices. There are certain practices related to being in the workforce, or in a marriage, or being a parent that will be common to many who occupy the same life situation and that will make this type of life situation structurally similar. But these practices are also different at different points in time, and they are also different depending on which cultural space one occupies. Being the male parent, for example, meant something quite different in the beginning of the 1900s compared to what it did towards the end of that century, as has been illustratively shown by Lissie Åström (1990) in her interview study of three-generational chains of Swedish men.

Thus one can say that each age cohort moves through these stages during their life course, producing a social rhythm that sweeps through and impacts on society, and gives it its specific character. This rhythm is, however, not symmetric and there is nothing that supports the idea that the generational rhythm should come in regular time intervals. When Ortega y Gasset was theorising the rhythm of ages, he thought of these rhythms as law-like forces of the historical process, a 'pulse-rate' with regular intervals where generations exchanged with almost mechanical precision. This idea of universal generations succeeding one another has proved difficult to support empirically, and 'the concrete results based on the theory of the universal pulse-rate of history are, of course, very modest' (Jaeger 1985: 283).

Such law-like generational exchanges can be contrasted with the more dynamic view on generations being successively formed in a *generationing* process; that is, the view on generations as a social formation that is moulded in relation to contextual factors in the same way as identity formation in the individual (Siibak & Vittadini 2012). The concept of generationing has been picked up from sociological research on children and childhood, where it was introduced by Leena Alanen (2001) as shorthand for the clumsier concept of 'generational structuring' (Alanen 2001: 129). Alanen's understanding of what constitutes a generation has been met with criticism, since it does not fully take into account the self-perception of generations as actuality that Mannheim emphasises (Närvänen & Näsman 2004: 80). However, that Alanen's use of the concept of generation is largely misleading does not automatically make her ideas of generationing as a process of generational becoming useless. In fact, it has been further theorised successfully by Italian media scholar Nicoletta Vittadini together with her Estonian colleague Andra Siibak (e.g. in Siibak & Vittadini 2012), and put to use in wider understandings of the formation of generations. In reference to Mannheim, they argue that the process of generationing is

> founded on historical events and the socio-techno-cultural milieu experienced in the formative years, as well as the development of the narrative of collective memories and frames of interpretation of "times"; and rituals and habits developed during the following stages of life.
>
> *(Siibak & Vittadini 2012: 3)*

Such rituals and habits also have their specific rhythms, although these are formed in social interaction in relation to the historical and technical contexts, and appear in less law-like forms.

So, although Ortega y Gasset and others who nourished the 'pulse-rate hypothesis' failed to convince, this does not mean that the concept of rhythm is entirely useless. The main problems with Ortega y Gasset and his student Julián Marías (1961/1970) are the totalising claims that they made regarding regularity of the historical process. Others have had more dynamic theories on social rhythms. French philosopher Henri Lefebvre (1992/2004) was, for example, also interested in rhythms: in his case rhythms produced at the intersection of an individual's meeting with a spatial structure (in Lefebvre's case the city). Lefebvre theorises three kinds of social rhythms: *polyrythmia*, as the bundles of rhythms that the human body and everyday life contains; *eurythmia*, as the harmonious interplay between the multitude of rhythms in everyday life; and *arrhythmia*, as the dissonance that occurs when different rhythms interact, producing a 'discordant' state (Lefebvre 1992/2004: 16). Rhythm, according to Lefebvre, is thus not in itself harmonious or disharmonious, but can be so in specific combinations and situations. The result of the interplay between these polyrhythms is what makes up everyday life in the social contexts of, for example, cities (or wherever there is social interaction). In essence Lefebvre's 'rhythmanalysis' can be read as a specific way of overcoming the classical structure–agency divide, just as is the case with Mannheim's theory of generations.

One could say that generations are formed through the eurythmic character of certain social formations, based on the fact that they share a historical location in time and space, and that the individuals in these formations acknowledge their situatedness as such, and thus form a generation as actuality. This includes identifying as a generation in relation to both younger and older generations, as has been pointed out by Fausto Colombo, who works with rhythmic metaphors in terms of a generational 'succession of waves', where the degree to which a specific generation leaves its impact on society will not only depend on its relation to the generation before or after, but also on the 'depth' of each generation: waves produced in deeper water also run deeper (Colombo 2011: 25). By analogy, some socio-historical events produce greater depth, and thus more pronounced waves, meaning that the generational consciousness will be stronger or more pronounced. In terms of rhythm one could say that the rhythm is more pronounced at certain points in history, while it is less so at other occasions.

The question most relevant in this context is what role the arrival of new media technologies, the development of new media genres, the rise of new media celebrities or the abrupt happenings of media events have in the process of generationing? Are they important enough to have an impact on the formation of generations to the extent that a concept of *media generations* is justified? Although much literature points to the media as important for the generational development of a generational consciousness, there are in fact few who hold the media as the most important factor. Notably, Gumpert and Cathcart (1985) theorised media grammars and how this specific form of literacy leaves its mark on the generational experience, but they never used the actual concept of media generations. The concept appears in several publications but is usually applied in a loose way, without any explicit definition (e.g. Bolin 2014c, Lepa et al. 2014). In fact, Andreas Hepp and his colleagues (Hepp, Berg & Roitsch 2015), in a study of media use among elderly people, make the only serious attempt at a definition (cf. also Hepp et al. 2014: 22ff):

> A media generation can be defined as a thickening of an age group or several age groups of people who, in their appropriation of media, share a specific space of experiencing mediatisation as well as a generational self-understanding as a media generation which is based in their media biography.
>
> *(Hepp, Berg & Roitsch 2015: 21, translation from German by Hepp)*

This definition lies well in line with the perspective adopted in this book, where the processual nature of generationing is emphasised. Hepp and his colleagues stress the relation to the broader process of mediatisation rather than the relation to individual media technologies, thus avoiding the difficult question about how a single medium can be defining for certain generations, in the way that has been done in previous research, and, above all, in the popular discourse of 'Facebook generations', and so on. It is more a question of how a certain group of people are situated in the media context in its totality, and how this totality produces responses that are founded in this experience. We shall, however, leave open for the moment the more detailed discussion of Hepp's and his colleagues' definition as well as questions of whether the impact of the media (in its totality) on generational formation is strong enough to merit the labelling of media generations. This discussion will be revisited in the final chapter of this book.

Conclusions

This chapter has aimed to establish a theoretical and analytical model for the understanding of the role of the media in the formation of generations. Based on the discussion in Chapter 1 on the processual nature of generationing and the forming of generations as social formations, this model has emphasised the interrelation between age (including ageing and memory formation), cohort, life phase and life situation factors as these interrelations are played out in the context of social and cultural circumstances. These relations have been exemplified through an empirical case of news media preferences, and the theoretical implications of the conceptual model will shortly be discussed. In the next three chapters this model will be put to work more thoroughly in relation to empirical examples, and the role of the media will be especially addressed.

3

GENERATION AS LOCATION

Media landscapes and generations

From the previous chapters we have learnt that one might expect that people born around the same time, and in the same specific geo-cultural and political environment, have the potential to develop similar relationships to the media as technologies and content. To Mannheim, a prerequisite for the forming of a generation is that people actually have experienced the same societal events, that they have a 'common location in the historical dimension of the social process' (Mannheim 1928/1952: 290). The condition for such experiences is that individuals are born at approximately the same time, and thus have the possibility of first-hand experience of societal events of historical magnitude, but also first-hand experience of fresh contact with new media forms and technologies. Only then is there a potential for developing a collective consciousness that binds individuals together through shared experience.

Each potential generation is born into a different media landscape. There will be media that are already established at the point of birth, and that all individuals take for granted and act naturally in relation to. And new media forms, genres and styles will develop, as well as new technological platforms that each individual will encounter during their life course. This is especially so for those born during the twentieth century, and one could argue that the constant transformation of the media landscapes that we inhabit is also one of the formative features of (late) modernity. Some of these transformations will be more dramatic than others, and will have a larger impact on the formation of generational consciousness. But the dominant mode is constant novelty, the increased speed at which technologies become renewed and where the digitisation process that all media and most other technologies have undergone virtually melts all that is solid into air, to paraphrase Marx, and to point to the formative features of modernity itself, as theorised eloquently by Marshall Berman (1982/1988).

But what would a media landscape that painted the picture of modernity look like? And what would it mean to be born into such a landscape? This chapter will outline the contours of such a landscape, that is, a structure that can form the basis for potential generations to experience, and thus possibly develop. The next section will account for the concept of media landscape. The following section will then situate potential generations in this landscape, and discuss a tentative way to close in on how group cohorts orient themselves in those landscapes.

Media landscapes

A metaphor for the media landscape is often used to describe the mediatised space in which people live and act. It is a spatial metaphor that indicates a phenomeno-logical 'world' perspective, just like the metaphor of the media environment. It first appeared as a technical term for painters, and was thus from the start connected to representational practices (cf. Adams 1994). Geographical landscapes are, however, also formed by individual or collective subjects, acting on the surrounding physical environment. Thus, a landscape is something that is represented for us (Casey 2004), shaped by someone, for some purpose: something that is *cultivated* into different shapes and forms (cf. Mels 1999). The *Encyclopædia Britannica Online* (see Bolin 2003: 18) also refers to it as an area of activity, which adds a three-dimensional aspect to the metaphor. It is thus both something constructed for us by, for example, a landscapist, painting the colours and the contours of the world for us, but it can also be a space shaped by the hands of a landscaper or a gardener, in which we can act – individually as well as socially together with others. And our actions in a landscape also impact on it. People may not always follow the paths through a garden, but make short-cuts over the lawn, producing a path not privileged by the gardener, similar to how one can produce a reading not privileged by a text (Hall 1973). Eventually such actions impact on the landscape itself. The metaphor of landscape, in short, allows for thinking about the media in a way that transgresses the structure–agency dichotomy and makes it possible to see action as structured by frameworks produced in previous social action, by preceding others. Those structures, however, never make individual action determined.

If we adopt this metaphor for the media and think of media landscapes, then there are two kinds of formative structures into which individual subjects are born: those of technological relations and those of representations.

First, when it comes to the structures of the media technologies themselves, these make up a technological terrain – electronic geographies in which individuals orient themselves in their everyday lives. These are the structures of how the media are organised technologically. Such 'media infrastructures' are described by Lisa Parks as 'the material sites and objects involved in local, national and/or global distribution of audiovisual signals and data [that] include phenomena such as broadcast transmitters, transoceanic cables, satellite earth stations, mobile telephone towers, and Internet data centres' (Parks 2015: 356). They are the material structures of the media – the material base, to make an analogy in Marxist terminology. This material base is distributed in space in the form of technological systems, sometimes visible to us in the form of telephone wires in the sky, which changed the character of the urban landscape dramatically around the end of the 1800s (Garnert 2005: 87ff), or satellite dishes towards the end of the 1900s (Parks 2012).

However, not all of these systems are visible; at least, some are hard to observe. For example, we might observe the television aerials or satellite dishes on the roofs of our houses, but we have a harder time observing the waves in the air although we know that they are there, allowing our television sets to work (and in the increasing wireless communication via personal and mobile laptops, tablets and mobile phones, the visible signs of connectivity gradually disappear). And although the satellite dishes are intended for receiving signals for our television sets, they in themselves make up what Charlotte Brunsdon (1991) has termed 'landscapes of taste', which signal cultural and class belonging. Although not always visible to us, the technological landscapes have a material dimension that makes them differ a bit from the symbolic landscapes. Their consequences are more determining in that technology and the organisation of technology only allows for the actions it is designed for. For example, early radio and television did not allow for listening to or watching programmes at a time chosen by the user, since they did not have storage and playback functions. One had to obey the time that was allotted by the broadcaster. The radio and television sets also did not allow for mobility, but were fixed entities that had an impact on the ways in which we structured our domestic environments, our homes (cf. Kleberg 1994, Spigel 1992).

Second are the media landscapes that result from representational practices. Through the production of accounts, images and representations a semiotic web is constructed, a map in which we can act as individuals, but which also sets up limits, privileges certain kinds of actions before others, and guides us in our everyday lives. Each account of the world, each such map, pursues its own argumentation vis-à-vis the surrounding world, and these accounts will have impacts on it. Each of these maps is also firmly anchored in its own historical setting, and in the present we can only act towards them historically. When the author August Strindberg writes a description of telephone lines along the rooftops in Stockholm (that is, a techno-logical structure), he is engaged in a representational practice, producing a map over a technological structure. However, the referent of this represented reality is not accessible for us today as terrain, only as a map (cf. Garnert 2005: 112 and 145ff).

Through the media and their representations, we learn of places we have never been, some of which we will never visit (for example, since they concern past his-torical situations which we can only revisit as maps, not as terrain). These media texts make up landscapes saturated with ideas, values, apprehensions. All of these kinds of mediated landscapes are laden with ideology, just as landscape paintings are ideological:

> Landscape […] is an instrument of cultural power, perhaps even an agent of power that is (or frequently represents itself as) independent of human inten-tions. Landscape as a cultural medium thus has a double role with respect to something like ideology: it naturalises a cultural and social construction, representing an artificial world as if it were simply given and inevitable, and

it also makes that representation operational by interpellating its beholder in some more or less determinate relation to its givenness as sight and site.

(Mitchell 1994/2002: 1f)

The one problematic issue in this quote is the word 'artificial'. Symbolic landscapes are no less real than material, geographical landscapes. Symbolic landscapes are indeed ideological, both as constructs and as constructors of social reality. The ways in which things are represented will inevitably have consequences, not only for how society is perceived in the present but also for how it will be in the future. Representations are, then, both descriptive and prescriptive.

The symbolic landscape of the media, as both technology and representation, primarily talks to our visual and aural senses. As such, the impact on our actions is not as direct and determining, but it is not always as obvious either. The capacity of the media to naturalise what they represent makes the landscapes that they produce much harder to identify and, therefore, also to resist. We are not always aware of the impact of the symbolic landscape in the same obvious way as we are of more manifest, physical ones. Physical landscapes are structured with roads, cities, bridges and canals, which privilege certain types of movement and action before others. In a similar way, the symbolic landscapes of technology and content also structure action by making some kinds of actions more probable than others. The architecture of urban landscaping, for example, has its correspondence in the landscaping of the symbolic surroundings, in the architecture of the media.

Potential generations in 'objective' media landscapes

If we, against the background of the idea of media landscapes, think of societal and media development in linear terms, focusing on these formative moments in modernity, or late modernity, we can construct a timeline in which media technologies appear successively over the years. Naturally, there will be national variations to these landscapes because some countries will have introduced, for example, television earlier than others. However, each potential generation will, in its specific national setting, appear at certain points on this timeline, and each will be historically situated in a time where some media technologies are already present while others appear during the course of their lives. An 'objective' structure of the media landscape that potential generations are born into is outlined in Figure 3.1.

Figure 3.1 indicates approximately the time at which certain media technologies are introduced. The specific time for the introduction of these in Sweden will vary depending on which geo-cultural region we are in, as, for example, television arrived earlier in larger cities than it did in the northern rural areas, but they would still make up a structure in which social action is carried out. Figure 3.1 is meant to give a rough outline of the technological part of the Swedish media landscape: that is, the techno-media landscape into which Swedish citizens of all ages are born. At the end of the nineteenth and the beginning of the twentieth century, communication technologies such as the telegraph and the telephone had already

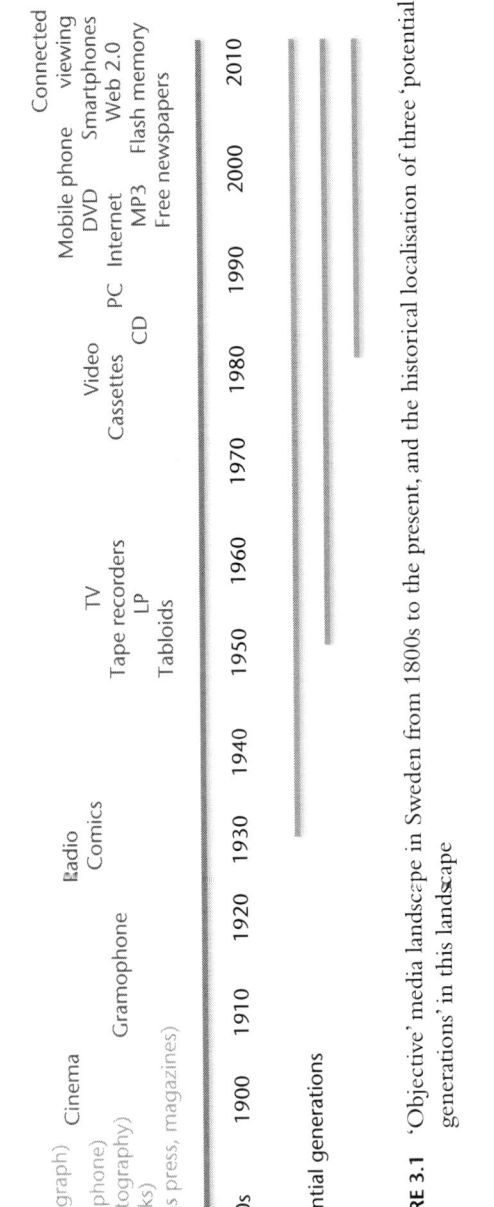

FIGURE 3.1 'Objective' media landscape in Sweden from 1800s to the present, and the historical localisation of three 'potential generations' in this landscape

been established, as had established media such as literature, photography, the mass press, cinema and soon the gramophone. It is worth noting that the circulation of newspapers was very high in Sweden and its fellow north-European countries such as Norway, Denmark and Estonia – in the 1970s and 1980s Sweden was among the top ten in the world (Opermann 2014: 77). Radio was introduced in Sweden in 1925, and it spread rapidly within the population. Within two decades more than two million households had acquired their own radio (Hadenius et al., 2008). For people born after 1925, radio was accordingly a medium that was already there as a natural given. Television was introduced to the public in 1956, and the spread of this medium was even more explosive. Within five years, 1.5 million households had bought a TV set. Within 20 years television had been firmly 'domesticated' and was found in three million Swedish living rooms. The domestication process as theorised by Roger Silverstone and colleagues (Silverstone et al, 1992, Haddon 2004) suggests an explanation for how media and other technologies are naturalised in households, but as I have argued elsewhere (Bolin 2010) it can also be used on a national level to understand how a media technology successively becomes appropriated, objectified, incorporated and conversed to having a natural place in the national context. For those born in the early 1950s, television was an arriving medium that became established and domesticated during their formative years in youth. The diffusion on a household level has since further developed, with more TV sets acquired within the same households, and television has become a personal medium rather than a family medium (Carlsson & Facht 2007: 263). This means that television is also a medium that does not really have a formative impact at one single point in time, but leaves its mark on several generations. Digital media, most notably computers and mobile phones, were introduced in the 1980s and they spread more widely to the Swedish public during the 1990s. In 1994, about 20 per cent of Swedish households possessed a computer, and the figure was similar for mobile phones. There followed a rapid increase until the early twenty-first century, when the growth had reached about 70 per cent for computers and 80 per cent for mobile phones. The Internet also showed a rapid diffusion during this time (Bergström 2005). For those born in the early 1980s, digital media (personal computers, mobile phones) were established during their formative teenage years. Just like television, 'digital media' are far from a unitary phenomenon and there are naturally several significant technological features related to these media.

The dominant twentieth century media – radio, television, the printed press – are largely rooted in the nation. Although international press and international radio stations do exist, these media are in their organisational form mainly national and are distributed in domestic languages. They are dominant in the sense that even those who do not subscribe to a daily newspaper or have a radio or television will be affected by their presence, which is in line with McLuhan's (1964) dictum that 'the medium is the message'. Once these media are domesticated in the national setting, they impact on all of the people living in their landscape. Towards the end of the twentieth century this will change, but for those who grew up before that time, the national media landscapes are relatively homogeneous.

In this landscape we can then situate age cohorts as potential generations, for example people born in the early 1930s, the early 1950s and the early 1980s. These cohorts, born around the same time and within the same national context, can be expected to encounter both old and new media in a similar way. The timeline can thus be used to situate and tentatively explore certain possible experiential contexts for certain age cohorts. For example, which media technologies and contents were already there when they were born? Which media appeared during their formative years? And at what age did they encounter novelties in the media landscape? This can then be used for empirical testing with survey data on media access, use, preferences or attitudes in order to see if there are consistencies in the ways in which certain age cohorts use or relate to the media. Figure 3.2 below gives an example of how these three cohorts as potential generations relate to mobile phone use over time.

Figure 3.2 shows how people with access to their own mobile phone use different functions on their mobiles between 2003 and 2013. We can see that there is internal consistency *within* each tentative generation, and that each cohort also differs from the other two. As can be expected, all cohorts increase their use of the three functions of talking, sending text messages and sending pictures on their mobiles over the years. But when combining the three functions, one can see that while the youngest cohort, born in the early to mid-1980s, takes full advantage of all functions, this is less so with those born in the early to mid-1950s, who in turn take more advantage of them than do the oldest cohort born in the early and mid-1930s.

That each cohort is not 'stable' in its use, in the meaning that older people should not be expected to engage in any new features, is by no means strange because no

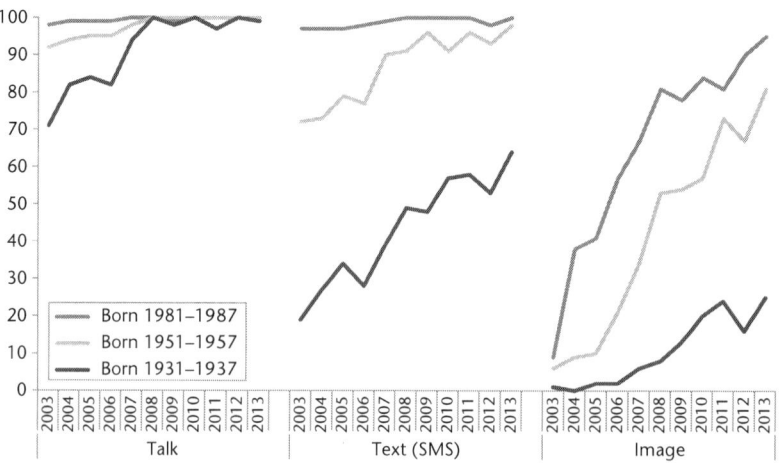

FIGURE 3.2 Generation as location: three Swedish age cohorts and their use of three functions on the mobile phone 2003–2013. 'Use' defined as 'use at all'

Source: Bolin (2014a: 235).

cohort exists in isolation from the others. Indeed, one can expect generational cohorts to be influenced by each other. There is in fact always a kind of what could be called inter-generational transmission that goes both ways. As Mannheim argues, generations are always 'in a state of constant interaction' (Mannheim 1928/1952: 301). Thus one can argue in reference to Figure 3.2 that the user patterns of the young also influence the older cohorts, so that the 1950s cohort increasingly adopts the functions of texting, and – to a lesser extent – of sending images. Similarly, the oldest cohort, temporally more distant to the youngest cohort, also takes up these functions, but to an even lesser degree than the 1950s cohort does.

One can of course also see this in terms of diffusion theory (Rogers 2003), and claim that young people in general belong to the early adopters of new media technologies. Although there is some truth to this (and Rogers does indeed point out that this is more complex), we can – in this specific case – see that the 'laggards', as they are usually labelled, only 'catch up' with the younger user cohorts when it comes to talking and do not catch up with the other two forms of communication. Sending text messages and images is less taken advantage of, despite the fact that the technology allows for it. Arguably – and this is where diffusion theory falls short in explanation – this is particularly because the oldest cohort is not used to thinking of a telephone as a broad communication tool: instead, as the original name says, they think of it as a *mobile* telephone. This interpretation is further supported by the fact that almost one third of mobile owners in the oldest cohort had *never used their mobile at all* in 2003. Thus, technology is there and accessible, but it is not used. At this point in time, this cohort was aged between 66 and 72 years old, and was thus living in retirement (and therefore over the period this cohort travels further and further into retirement). As previous analysis has shown, people in retirement have – in general – a less mobile lifestyle (Bolin & Westlund 2009: 112ff), and as basically all people at this time in Sweden had access to landline phones (Bolin 2006a: 404), the force of habit would prompt retired people to choose the stationary landline before the mobile alternative. This could then be explained by a combination of belonging to a certain generation and being in a specific life stage, rather than being attributed to age in itself.

In accounts from the early days of a medium's entrance into the media landscape, it is often the technology in itself that leaves the strongest mark. An interview study by Swedish media researcher Birgitta Höijer (1998) accounted for several such instances where 'the medium is the message' (McLuhan 1964). In the early days of radio, for example, the occasion of listening for the first time was an event in itself. Höijer has several quotes related to this; for example, the following account of an older female informant recalling the first time she heard radio in the 1920s:

> My father and I were out walking one Sunday, and we met a police inspec-tor that my father knew. 'We have been equipped with a radio down at the station', he said. 'Oh, really?', said my father. 'Do you want to come in and listen?', he said. 'Yes, yes!' Of course we would like to do that. It was very exciting. It was a big event in my life.
>
> *(Höijer 1998: 46)*

However, as radio (and other media) become domesticated and naturalised as technologies, memories tend to centre on genres and content instead. The technological landscape thus needs to be coupled with a symbolic, representational landscape of media genres and content. We can thus build further on the landscape as represented in Figure 3.1 and add the main milestones in content development. Figure 3.3 outlines some major generic events, such as radio stations (Radio Nord, Radio Luxembourg), significant artists (Beatles, Elvis, Greta Garbo, Spice Girls) or sports stars (Björn Borg, Ingmar Stenmark), but also programmes or programme series (*Karusellen, Bonanza, Hylands hörna, Bingolotto*).

Radio Nord was a pirate radio station, broadcasting popular music (as well as commercial advertising) from international waters in the Baltic Sea between 1961 and 1962. In 1962, this ultimately resulted in the launch of a new channel for popular music by Swedish Radio, which was the public service broadcaster and which had a monopoly on broadcasting. At different points in time artists from the cinema or music were hugely popular. For example, when sports stars were competing – like tennis champion Björn Borg playing the Wimbledon finals in the mid-1970s, or alpine ski racer Ingemar Stenmark skiing for World Cup medals around the same time – this was followed live on television and radio by most Swedes. Even for those who did not take part, these events could hardly go unnoticed because they were covered by all of the major news channels (print, radio, television). Such media moments would also include ABBA winning the Eurovision Song Contest in 1974. There were also some notable radio and television serials of the time that had the same popular appeal among audiences. For example, radio show *Karusellen* was broadcast in the 1950s and was led by the immensely popular host Lennart Hyland, who also developed this into the radio show *Hylands hörna* in 1961 in order then to take *Hylands hörna* to television in 1962, where it became a hugely popular Saturday evening show for many years afterwards.

These are naturally all examples of hugely popular shows in the media, and one could easily add more similar examples to these. To the timeline should also be added *news events* with widespread reporting in national media. For Sweden (and many other countries, cf. Volkmer 2006a), such news moments would include both *international events* related to the two world wars, of course, but also the Vietnam war, the building and destruction of the Berlin wall, the Cold War and the space race, the murder of J.F. Kennedy, the death of Princess Diana, the terrorist attack of 11 September 2001, and other widely reported news events. In addition there are also *national events* of importance: the military killing of five people in connection to a strike in Ådalen in 1931, the murder of Prime Minister Olof Palme in 1985, the Soviet submarine U137 running aground in Swedish waters in 1981, the shipwreck disaster of MS Estonia in 1994, and so on. These are all events that were widely reported in the news media, and set the news agenda for all national news media.

The fact that these events and features were widely reported, or have in hindsight been deemed to be formative moments in the history of Swedish media, does not say anything about how they were perceived, interpreted and experienced by

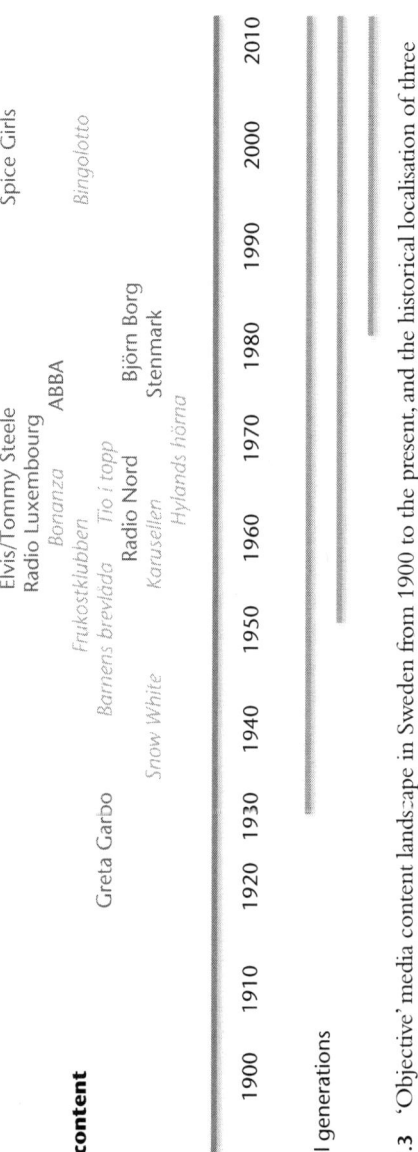

FIGURE 3.3 'Objective' media content landscape in Sweden from 1900 to the present, and the historical localisation of three 'potential generations' in this landscape

individual media users. In order to discover this, other methods have to be taken into consideration, and this will be explored more deeply in the next chapter. There are, however, other factors that can be considered with respect to how certain cohorts can be located in the historical process, such as the cultural context of representations and the events referred to.

Locating cohorts in cross-cultural and cross-national settings

It is easy to judge all trends in media access and use against the media landscape of one's own – in this case, Swedish – media landscape. This was for the better part of the 1900s a fairly homogeneous landscape, and even if there were local or regional differences – for example, television arriving earlier in the southern parts of Sweden and in the big cities compared to the rural northern parts – the representational and organisational structure of the media has been fairly similar.

However, if one compares access and use over cross-national settings, some unexpected nuances can be revealed in patterns of use and access. If we, for example, compare Sweden with one of its neighbouring countries, such as Estonia, then interesting similarities and differences appear, which shed light on the specificities of the respective countries. Compared to Sweden, radio, television and digital media were introduced in Estonia at approximately the same time (Opermann 2014: 75ff), which means that technologically, the two countries are similar when it comes to introduction of media technologies. There are, however, differences when it comes to speed of dissemination, the content structures provided, and the general geo-political and historical context. The specific content dimension will mainly be left for the next chapter to discuss, while this section will focus on some of the similarities and differences related to dissemination and historical organisation of the media, in order to then focus on some of the empiric differences related to media access and use that can help locate Estonian – and Swedish – media users in their media landscape.

The point of this comparison is that Sweden has been a stable democracy and a welfare state for many years (compared with the much shorter democratic experiences of Estonia). Sweden's market economy has a long history, and consumer society was firmly established in Sweden long before it arrived in Estonia. As a nation-state, Estonia was independent for the first time between 1918 and 1940, and was then independent from 1991 onwards following the collapse of the Soviet Union. In the early 1990s, living standards and purchasing power were very low compared to neighbouring countries such as Finland and Sweden, which had longer histories of market economy participation. When Estonia regained its independence, its government soon set out to restructure the country in several ways. The country's first Prime Minister, Mart Laar, launched an economic policy that he considered to be a 'shock therapy' (Laar, 2007). Politically and culturally, the nation strove to 'return to the Western world' (Lauristin and Vihalemm, 1997). Economic restructuring was, however, but one part of the reformation programme. One aim of the post-1991 reforms in Estonia was thus to 'catch up' with the modernisation processes in the

West. The goal of bringing Estonia into post-modernity through digital technology was implemented through projects such as the Tiger's Leap campaign, initiated by the Ministry of Education in 1997 to enhance 'the educational system in Estonia in the rapidly changing world with introduction of modern information and communication technology',[1] thus promoting computer literacy among Estonian schoolchildren (see also Runnel et al., 2009). This application of the 'leap-frog' process (Howard, 2007) included additional education for teachers as well as the large-scale introduction of computers into schools.[2]

The Tiger's Leap campaign, along with other efforts to introduce and establish ICTs in Estonia, were specific cultural technologies that were adopted to reach political, economic and social goals, and to restructure Estonia in a globalized world at the time that Estonia was working to enter the European Union. As is the case with all cultural technologies, ICTs are strongly embedded within the broader context of historically grounded cultural perceptions, values and discourses that all affect the ways in which a specific technology might be used in a particular cultural and historical context.

When it comes to the history of the media, there are some shared features that unite Sweden and Estonia (e.g. the introduction of the mass media at approximately the same time), but there are also substantial differences. This makes a good starting point for cross-cultural comparisons. To compare phenomena across cultures is a methodological strategy that helps point to the cultural specificities of global or trans-national phenomena. An interesting example in this respect is mobile telephony. Since mobile technology is disseminated on a global basis, this comparative strategy is specifically beneficial for evaluating the dissemination and usage of mobile phones in Estonia.

The introduction of mobile telephony in Estonia should be evaluated in relation to the already existing media landscape, including landline telephony. Shortly after independence in 1991, landline phone penetration in Estonia was 44 per cent, radio 69 per cent and colour television sets 69 per cent (BMF, 1994). Comparable figures for Sweden were all between 95 and 100 per cent (Kratz 1994). So even if the introduction of technology is simultaneous, economic, political and historical circumstances have made dissemination in Estonia slower. Figure 3.4 summarises the comparative diffusion of mobile phones in Estonia and Sweden between 1993 (when the first survey was made of mobile telephony in Estonia) and 2008 (when access is on the same level as Sweden).

In Estonia, access to mobile phones initially increased quite slowly: from just one per cent in 1993 to seven per cent in 1997, followed by a dramatic increase in access over the two years from 1997 to 1999, where almost half of the Estonian population became owners of mobile phones. In comparison, the increase in mobile phone ownership in Sweden was more gradual. This dramatic increase in Estonia can be explained partly by increased income levels (from an average monthly income of the equivalent of 81 USD in 1993 to 262 USD in 1999), making it more affordable to buy a mobile phone, but it can also be related to the fact that the landline phone had never become firmly domesticated in the Estonian households.[3] In 1993, when mobile phones were introduced on the Estonian market, landline penetration was around 44 per cent. Landline access then rose to 60 per cent in 2002, and then stagnated until 2007 (ITU 2009: 24). It then slowly decreased again, at the same time

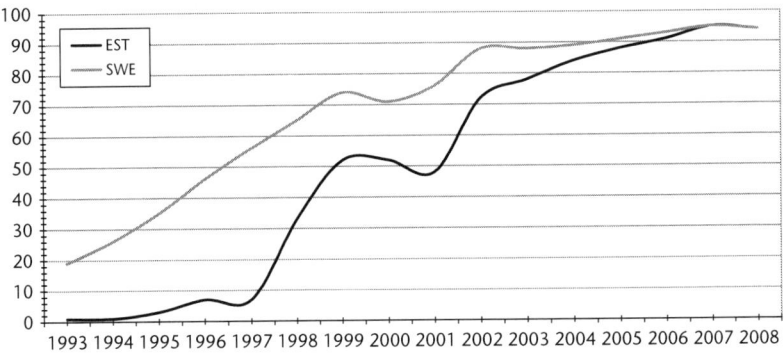

FIGURE 3.4 Percentage of ownership of mobile phones in Estonia and Sweden, 1993–2008

Source: Estonian data are from Runnel et al. (2006), from the Variable Media Landscapes project and ITU (for the years 2001 and 2003). Swedish data are from the SOM Institute surveys.[4]

TABLE 3.1 Landline ownership and abandonment among mobile owners in Estonia and Sweden, 2002 (per cent)

	Never had a landline phone	*Have given up the landline phone due to mobile phone access*	*N*
Estonia	12.6	16.6	1022
Sweden	1.2	1.6	1127

Source: Variable Media Landscapes 2002.

as mobile penetration increased. Clearly, many Estonians exchanged their landline phones for mobile subscriptions. In that sense, the mobile was not as much a complement to the landline as it was in Sweden because many Estonians either never had landline or gave it up when acquiring a mobile. Table 3.1 shows the difference to Swedish mobile owners at the time when Estonian landline subscription peaked.

As can be seen from Table 3.1, Estonians were far more likely to have given up their landline phones after gaining access to mobiles than were Swedes. At the same time, Swedes were far more likely to have had landlines in the first place. That is, the landline was more domesticated as a technology in Sweden than it was in Estonia, accounting at least in part for the dramatic rise in mobile phone adoption in Estonia in the late 1990s.

The pattern in Sweden seems, contrary to Estonia, to be to not give up one's landline subscription. The trend in Sweden is rather a phasing out of landline telephony, where people have access through their families while they grow up, but when they move away from home and create their own household, landline telephony is not an option, since all young people from around the age of 9 to 10 have a mobile phone. Figure 3.5 shows how this 'wave' of non-landline users has grown each year.

Figure 3.5 deals with age cohorts, and we can see that most individuals in the youngest cohort, who are 16–19 years old at the point of measurement, have access to landline phones since they still live with their parents. Gradually, over the years access

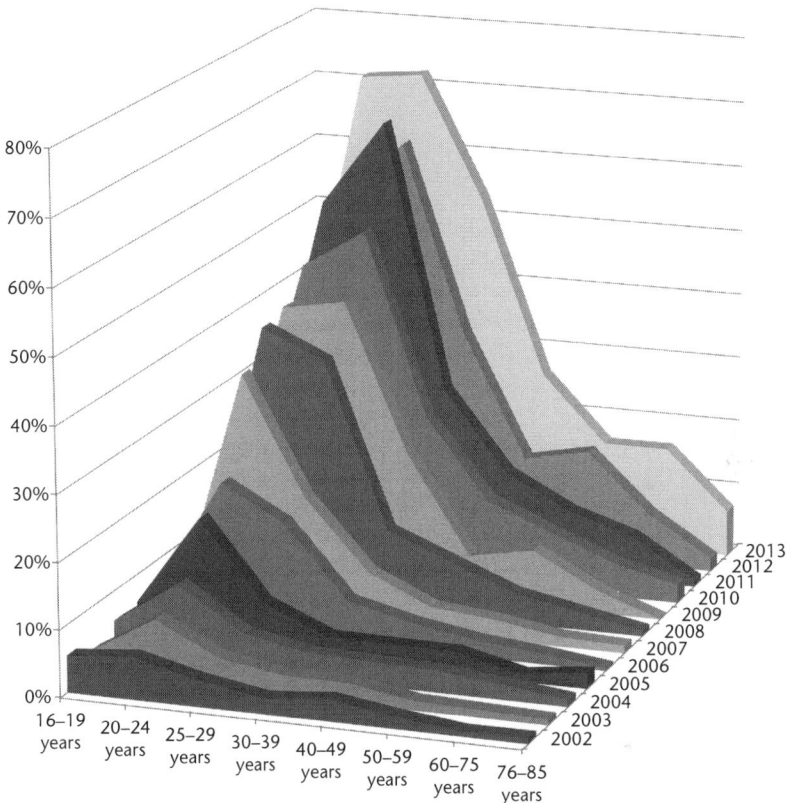

FIGURE 3.5 Non-access to landline telephones in different age groups in Sweden, 2002–2013

Source: The National SOM Surveys 2002–2013.

to landline phones decreases for the age groups of 20–24 and 25–29 years: that is, the age at which most people move away from home in Sweden. Moreover, the abandonment of the landline phone among those cohorts persists. That is, these cohorts do not 'go back' to using a landline telephone when they grow older. The fact that young people have been using mobile phones since around the age of 10 in Sweden, combined with the long-term strategy of telephone service providers to phase out landline telephony makes going back more difficult and costly, and we can thus predict that the wave of non-access to landline subscriptions will follow the trend seen in Figure 3.5.

From a generational perspective this is interesting since it illustrates how age and life-course factors ultimately also result in generational effects. What starts as an effect of age and a change in life situation or life stage soon establishes itself as a common pattern shared by peers of the same age. The shared experience among those in the same life situation will separate them from their parents' generation, that is, those who were brought up with the landline phone. Despite having smartphones for some time, the parents' (and grandparents') generation still cling on to their landline subscription. This makes the young cohorts' relation to the landline different compared to that of their parents, and this specific approach to the landline creates common ground for a potential generational user pattern to grow.

The formation of generational user habits

Given the different historical backgrounds of Sweden and Estonia, one could expect that cohorts brought up in these two somewhat different media landscapes would differ in their behaviours related to new and arriving media, similar to how different age cohorts related to the 'emerging consumer culture' in the context of the 'transitional cultural condition' in Estonia after independence in 1991 (Kalmus et al. 2009). Veronika Kalmus and her colleagues found that there is a persistence in the consumer pattern produced by what can be called the choice of necessity that has lived on among older people brought up under Soviet consumer culture. In their survey, they found that respondents born in 1960 or earlier were more marked by the scarcity and restrictions in choice compared to those Estonians who grew up after independence into a consumer society and were characterised by 'a high level of appropriation of commercially produced and branded goods and services, as well as the related values in their life-world' (Kalmus et al. 2009: 69). In a similar way, one can expect people who have developed user patterns under certain media conditions to bring these patterns with them into new media landscapes.

This, however, presupposes that these patterns have been firmly established. An interesting case that points to how the degree to which the media have been established can be found if one compares Swedish and Estonian young people brought up in similar circumstances of consumption – that is, having access to the same technology – but where tenacious historical structures might influence media use in the present – for example, related to the mobile phone. This is a possible explanation for why Estonian young people between the ages of 18 and 24 have very different user patterns when it comes to the two most frequently used functions on the mobile: texting and talking (as can be seen in Figure 3.6). While Swedish young people use the phone equally for texting and talking on a daily basis, Estonian young people of the same cohort are more likely to talk than text.

The sample is made up of respondents in their formative years between age 18 and 24. At the point of the first measure, in 2002, this means that this cohort was born between 1978 and 1984, towards the end of the Soviet occupation of Estonia.[5] Since most of this group were very young during the Soviet era, they most likely have only vague memories from that time. There are very small differences between the countries when it comes to access to mobiles for these age groups during these years, although there are clearer differences for the populations as a whole (cf. Figure 3.3). In these age groups access is 93 and 96 per cent for Estonia and Sweden, respectively, in 2002 and over 98 per cent for both countries from 2006 onwards. This means that basically all young people have access to mobiles. Despite this, the differences between Swedish and Estonian youth resemble those between the youngest and the two older cohorts in Figure 3.2.

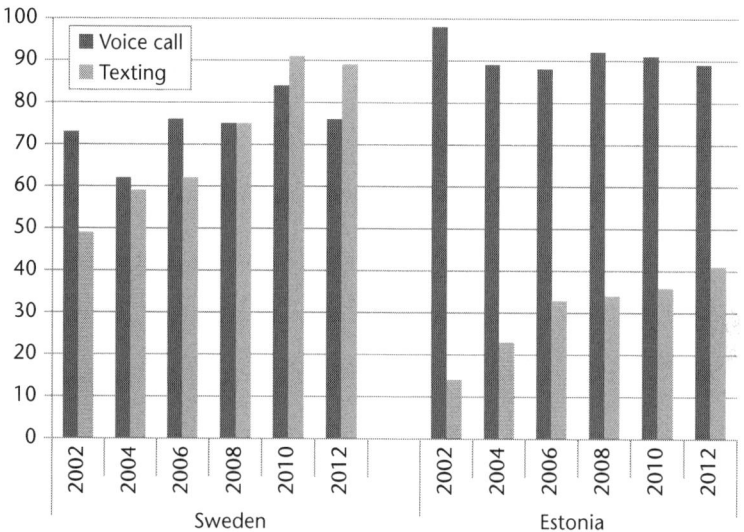

FIGURE 3.6   Percentage of Estonians and Swedes aged 18–24 years old using text and voice mobile functions daily, 2002–2012

Source: Data from the Variable Media Landscapes project (2002–2012).[6]

A possible explanation for the different patterns could be found in relation to different pricing structures, but that does not seem to be the case (Bolin 2010: 67). More convincingly, the differences in levels of talking versus texting on mobiles by Estonian and Swedish young adults is explained by the specific historical-cultural context of mobile and landline technology in Estonia, and the way in which it differs from how mobile technology was domesticated in Sweden. In this respect, the pattern in Sweden is more in line with other countries where fixed-line penetration was high at the moment when the mobile phone entered the landscape, for example Japan and the United States (Baron & Hård af Segerstad 2010). If one compares the texting versus talking pattern across these four nations and for the same age groups one can see that Estonian youth clearly differ from youth in the other three national contexts.

While Table 3.2 reveals quite different texting volumes between Swedish, Japanese and US youth, the relation between texting and voice calling is the same – all youth in these countries text far more than they speak over the mobile. The opposite is true for Estonian youth at this point in time, where those who make frequent calls (>20 calls per day) dominate over those who text frequently.

The rapid growth of access to mobile telephony in Estonia has (see Figure 3.3), to a certain extent, made the landline phone superfluous – at least among parts of the Estonian population. In 2008, access to landline phones had declined to 54 per cent of the population, from having been 60 per cent in 2002.[7] This trend is well in

TABLE 3.2 Percentage of Estonians, Swedes, Americans and Japanese aged 18–24 years old sending and/or receiving more than 20 voice calls or 20 text messages per day, 2007–2008

	Estonia	Sweden	US	Japan
Voice	7.5	3.8	2.5	0.6
Text	2.5	9.2	17.8	26.8
N	161	132	523	529

Source: Estonian data are from the Variable Media Landscapes Project for the year 2008,[8] and Swedish data from the national SOM Institute survey for the year 2008. US and Japanese data, collected in 2007–2008, are from Baron and Hård af Segerstad (2010).

line with developments in other 'transition countries' in the post-Soviet area where fixed-line penetration was much lower than in Western Europe (Vagliasindi et al. 2006). This finding suggests that in Estonia the fixed-line telephony was not fully domesticated on a national level and, hence, the mobile phone easily took over as the main medium for voice communication. By contrast, in Sweden, the penetration of landline telephony has been close to 100 per cent since the 1970s, and Sweden has long been one of the countries with the highest landline penetration in the world.[9] Since Swedes have a longer history of widespread access to landline phones, they have seemingly been more prone to retaining the older technology, arguably because it has been more firmly domesticated and taken for granted in the Swedish household setting. Admittedly, among today's young Swedish adults it is becoming less common to subscribe to a landline phone when one moves away from one's parents' home to an independent residence. But this development is quite slow despite the fact that the telephone providers encourage the phasing out of landline technology. This mainly follows a life stage pattern where young people never take up fixed line subscriptions when moving away from their parents (see Figure 3.5).

This is further supported by the fact that most Swedes in the youngest cohort, aged 15–19 years old, have access to landline phones and, hence, can choose to use landlines for talking (at their parents' expense), whereas this option is not available for many Estonians in the same cohort. In fact, in 2002, 40 per cent of Estonian youth aged 18–24 did not have access to landline telephony in their homes (whereas 93 per cent had access to a mobile). Only three per cent of Swedish 18–24 year-olds shared this position.

So, in conclusion to this example of cultural comparison one can establish that even if two countries have a similar media landscape technologically, that does not mean that the people inhabiting those landscapes will act in the same way. The example clearly shows that the ways in which Estonian young people have appropriated the mobile differs substantially from the ways that the gadget has been used in several other cultural settings (e.g. Sweden, the United States, and Japan). We can expect that historical traditions and habits will affect use in the present, and we can also expect development to follow life stage patterns, as is the case with the slow disappearance of landline telephony in Sweden.

The stronger 'domestic status' of the landline phone in Sweden has meant that Swedes generally have access to *both* landline and mobile telephony, whereas this is not the case in Estonia, where Estonians have abandoned landline telephony at a faster pace than have Swedes. The diffusion of the mobile phone has been much faster and more intense in Estonia, as a country that entered into this process late. This conclusion is supported by the findings of Philip Howard (2007), who studied 200 countries and analysed the extent to which 'new information technologies can spread more quickly when [...] deep investment in a communications infrastructure has not been made' (Howard, 2007: 134, cf. Castells et al., 2007: 13). Howards speaks of 'investment' in terms of governmental engagement in infrastructural development, but one can also think of investment in cultural terms, such as those habits and practices that are developed in social use of the media.

Symbolic media landscapes

Media landscapes have thus far been discussed as technological structures, with the main example centred on mobile and landline telephony. However, technology is but one kind of (material) structure in relation to which birth cohorts act and develop understandings. If the material structures of technology can be said to make up a 'hard' structure, then there are also the 'soft' structures of discourse: that is, the symbolic media landscape. These landscapes are much harder to grasp, both for those living in them, and for the researcher in his or her analysis of them. The symbolic media landscape includes more general perceptions of historical development, reproduced in historical understandings of what a country 'is', and why it has developed the way it has. In line with this, there is a growth in general perceptions and cultural ideas of, for example, Sweden as a social democracy and welfare state, and Estonia as a small, post-communist nation with high-tech ambitions. Such perceptions range from the longer historical to the more contemporary understandings.

As Swedish media sociologist Jan Ekecrantz once pointed out, two cultural ideas about Estonia have shown remarkable consistency over the twentieth century: that of the *Hansa* (a celebration of commerce across borders), and that of the *Backyard* (the 'dangerous conditions beyond the border'). These ideas have been prevalent irrespective of whether Estonia has been independent or under Soviet rule (Ekecrantz 2004: 52). Historically, one could argue that these two ideas have their roots in different epochs, where the Hansa discourse is the older one that constructs a geo-political space grounded in the commercial connections between cities along the coast of the Baltic Sea, whereas the East as a construction of the Western Other is of later date. As Ekecrantz summarises, Estonia 'has been an unusually unstable time-space, repeatedly constructed and reconstructed in a more or less unbalanced interaction with surrounding spheres of power, in the last decade increasingly orienting itself towards Nordic politics and markets' (Ekecrantz 2004: 44).

When it comes to Western perceptions, Estonia has frequently been bundled together with other post-Soviet states, most often with its fellow Baltic neighbours Latvia and Lithuania. A native Estonian, however, might rather point out the differences, emphasising the sharp distances in language, for example. The Baltic States were always considered a 'Soviet West', where, in the words of Estonian media researcher Margit Keller, 'the Iron Curtain appear[ed] more transparent for those looking outwards' (Keller, 2005: 218). And it is often pointed out that the most transparent part of the curtain was alongside the northern Estonian border towards Finland, where Estonians were able to access Finnish television. Some of these perceptions were also encouraged in nation branding efforts after independence, forming discourses of a 'return to the Western world' (Lauristin & Vihalemm 1997), and other discursive approximations to Scandinavia and the EU. In the nation branding campaign, Brand Estonia was launched before the upcoming final of the Eurovision Song Contest in Tallinn in May 2002 with slogans such as 'Nordic with a twist', which were developed in order to alter 'the spatial understanding by marking distance towards the East (and the South Baltic neighbours)' (Bolin 2006b: 82).

These discursive constructions and the way in which Estonia is symbolically framed naturally have consequences for the way in which citizens of Estonia perceive their country, just as they have consequences for the image of Estonia in the eyes of citizens elsewhere in the world. As a contextual semiotic system, a discursive backdrop to people being born and raised in Estonia, it also has consequences for their self-understanding as Estonians of a specific generational belonging. In that sense, the symbolic context is just as important as the material environment.

Furthermore, in situations of transformation there also arise struggles over such symbolic constructions. It is a case in point that the efforts on the part of the Estonian government – and the branding agencies that they hired in order to change the image of Estonia in front of the rest of the world, around the Eurovision Song Contest final – were highly contested domestically, as has been shown in analyses of the campaign and its domestic reception (Jordan 2014).

The symbolic landscape is easier to observe in the transitional state of Estonia after the collapse of the Soviet Union, a condition the country shared with other post-Soviet countries. Undeniably, changes in the symbolic landscape – the actual changes in the content structures of the media across all technologies, including radio, press, literature, cinema and music – are easier to spot in times of transformation than they are in stable situations. The changes are manifest and easy to observe. In the post-Soviet situation after independence in 1991, this meant that there were also high aspirations for structuring this new and, in the case of Estonia, mainly commercial landscape that would replace the state-controlled media of Soviet times. Thus, the content in newspapers changed as journalists no longer had to 'write between the lines'. Commercials were introduced on radio and television, and a range of new radio stations and television channels were born. New business newspapers and magazines were introduced, not least because foreign media houses saw the opportunity to enter into new markets. In this new situation, an ideology of commercial media as the solution to the old, state-controlled media arose, where the main quality-marker of media content was that it was commercial (Bengtsson & Lundgren 2005).

Such abrupt changes in the symbolic landscape naturally impact on the generational formation for those whose developmental years occurred in the midst of the societal restructurings in Estonia. On the basis of quantitative data, Signe Opermann comes to the conclusion that what she calls 'the buffer generation', born between 1958 and 1971, displays ambivalence, but also a capacity for adjusting smoothly to new situations. Among the buffer generation, she concludes:

> a certain uncertainty can be noticed, which results from their life course, during which they encountered several abrupt social changes and radically reform their habits and principles. As known from the recent history of Soviet Estonia, this generation had to learn the lessons of conformism, through which they were transformed into 'normalised Soviet people' at a tender age. Thus, as also shown by the analysis, the so-called buffer generation is relatively flexible and ready to adopt new formats and technologies offered by the news media, while on the other hand they also preserve earlier behaviour patterns and repertoires and do not give them up so easily.
>
> *(Opermann 2014: 232)*

Such capabilities to adapt to new situations have also been discussed in youth cultural research, where, for example, Thomas Ziehe and Herbert Stubenrauch (1982) argued that youth in the 1970s were 'culturally released', meaning that they were released from the ties of tradition and were psychologically more adaptive regarding changed social demands connected to new societal and cultural conditions – just as the peasants in the beginning of the Industrial Revolution were 'set free' from their feudal binds and thus 'free' to sell their labour power, as theorised by Karl Marx in *Capital* (1867/1976: Chapter 25, Section 3). This 'setting free' (*Freisetzung*) was a precondition for the development of the labour market as a basis for industrialised capitalist commodity production, as it was built on the free exchange of commodities for a price set by buyer and seller. The 'freedom' gained by the proletariat also meant that they were 'freed' from control over their bodies as a means of production. One could possibly make an analogy here between the change from feudal to industrialised society, and the change from 'the socialist personality' to the capitalist and consumerist demands in market economy Estonia, where this generation is caught between two types of demands, producing adaptive personalities that are to be culturally released and at the disposal for the consumption market. A buffer generation finds itself in an ambivalent position here, being both 'set free' to consume, while having been brought up with the restrictions of the anti-consumption behaviour promoted in the socialist Soviet Union.

Conclusions

This chapter has analysed the ways in which generations are located in media landscapes, and the contextual features that are important for understanding similarities in approaches as well as differences. The main part of the chapter has discussed the technological landscapes, and the ways in which the media have been organised. From this chapter we can learn that generations who are similarly located in the historical process and the technological media landscape need not necessarily develop the same kinds of responses to arriving or existing media due to historical and geo-political circumstance. Hence, young people develop quite dissimilar user patterns of texting and voice calling in Japan, the United States, Sweden and Estonia; the user pattern in Estonia differs dramatically from the other three countries – something that can be explained by the quite specific nature of its historical media landscape, and the habits established around the landline telephone.

This chapter has also briefly addressed the symbolic, or representational landscapes and how these make up a reception context in which media users act. The symbolic media landscape also varies over the years, and different birth cohorts enter into this landscape at different points in time. To describe the symbolic landscape is, however, more difficult because the plurality of media content and information that makes up this landscape is much richer and thus much harder to describe in detail compared to the technological structure (although this chapter has hardly exhausted the features of the technological infrastructure either). The next chapter will discuss how media users relate to the surrounding media landscape in more detail, both when it comes to its technological constitution and to the way in which media content is structured.

Notes

1 Quoted from the Tiger's Leap campaign's now non-functioning web pages, available at www.tiigrihype.ee (accessed 2 July 2003).
2 See, for example, the historical account provided by the Tiger Leap's Foundation. Available at www.tiigrihype.ee/static/files/6.tiigrihype2007ENG_standard.pdf (accessed 1 November 2008).
3 More details around the introduction and establishment of mobile phones in Sweden and Estonia can be found in Bolin (2010).
4 Sampling in the Estonian studies and the Swedish study differed slightly with respect to age. The Estonian data for 1993–2000, and for 2002 and 2004, includes people between ages 15–74. For 2006 and 2008, the Estonia data includes people aged 15–85. All Swedish data are for people between ages 15–85.
5 The respondents in the 2004 survey were born between 1980 and 1986; those in the 2006 sample were born between 1982 and 1988; for the sample of 2008, the respondents were born between 1984 and 1990.
6 Sample size varied as follows for the age group 18–24 year-olds – 2002: Sweden 126–129 and Estonia 168–173; 2004: Sweden 127–129 and Estonia 182–186; 2006: Sweden 145–147 and Estonia 228; 2008: Sweden 102 and Estonia 161; 2010: Sweden 131 and Estonia 177–179; 2012: Sweden 88–89 and Estonia 136. The variation in sample size is explained by the fact that unequal numbers of respondents replied to each item. Thus, for example, 'Sweden 126–129' should be read as 126 respondents for calling and 129 for texting.
7 Figures are from the Variable Media Landscapes Project for the year 2008.
8 The figures from Estonia are based on the higher percentage for the answers to the two questions 'How often do you initiate voice calls/text messages per day?' and 'How often do you receive voice calls/text messages per day?' One can expect that those who send many messages/calls also receive many messages/calls and vice versa.
9 In the 1970s, Sweden had one of the highest levels of telephone penetration in the world, second only to the United States. See www.ericssonhistory.com/company/an-emerging-global-company/A-new-market-situation/1/(accessed 14 July 2015).

4

GENERATION AS ACTUALITY

Subjective landscapes of media generations

The previous chapter discussed generations as located in the media landscape, examined how the nature of this media landscapes and its historical and geo-political embedding affects the ways in which cohort-based user patterns develop, and asked how specific generational patterns of use can be discerned. It was shown how different cohorts, differently located in the historical process, develop different ways to relate to the media as technologies and as content, and how this can be analysed in terms of these cohorts being seen as potential generations.

While location in the temporal and spatial structures surrounding human existence was the basis for the previous chapter, this chapter will discuss the ways in which generations can also be actualised for themselves: that is, how people perceive their location in the social and media landscapes, and how such perceptions can be interpreted. A foundational premise for such a realisation is that people share experiences, and through these shared moments of commonality can create the 'we-sense' required for a generation to actualise. This chapter will start to approach the question on how such 'we-sense' occurs, and in what situations and contexts this specific collective identity is activated.

This chapter will continue the cross-generational and cross-cultural comparative approach that was presented in the previous chapter, and pick its main examples from a series of focus group interviews with Estonian and Swedish media users born in the early 1940s, early 1960s, late 1970s and early 1990s. The interviews were conducted in late 2011 and early 2012, and the groups were composed of people born around certain years in both countries, with a special focus on the transformations in society and the arrival of new media. The four focus groups can be placed along the time axis representing the 'objective' media landscape: that is, the landscape as defined through the actual appearance of diverse media technologies, the specific content in these media, and by significant historical events. This landscape is objective in the sense that these things occurred irrespective of whether or not they were mentioned by the respondents in the interviews. It has its own technological and semiotic rhythm, parallel to the social rhythm of events that occurred over the duration of the twentieth and twenty-first centuries. The media landscape provides the techno-semiotic and socio-historical circumstances into which the respondents were born, and shall be set in relation to the subjectively perceived media landscape: that is, the landscape as it is remembered and made meaningful by the respondents, the rhythms that are produced as a result of the meeting between the technological, the symbolic and the societal structure.

Each of these potential generations was born into a different media landscape and entered into the historical process at a specific point where some media technologies were already present, while others arrived during the course of their lifetime. The 'objective' structure is outlined in Figure 4.1 to illustrate the road along which each of these birth cohorts travelled through the media landscape, and to find which media technologies were already present and which arrived during the course of their lifetime.

The focus groups were constructed out of four tentative generations: that is, individuals born at a similar location in the historical process. These points, which will be described shortly, were chosen in order for the respondents to have their formative years around the time of media changes and/or supposedly formative societal conditions.[1] There were four to eight respondents in each group, and they were interviewed for around two hours each.

The oldest focus group consisted of people born in the beginning of the 1940s (1939–1946), in the midst of the Second World War, and who grew up in post-war Soviet Estonia and post-war Sweden. This generation was at the time of the interviews in early retirement, many of them had children as well as grandchildren. They had mixed work life experience and were originally brought up in different parts of the two countries. This (tentative) generation had grown up in a media landscape that was dominated by the mass media cinema, literature, press and radio. During their formative years they saw the arrival of television, tape recorders, tabloid press and the LP record. It should be noted, though, that even if television and music media *technologically* were the same in Sweden and Estonia, the *content* was dramatically different (which of course also goes for the press, cinema, etc.). They were still very young at the end of the Second World War, but they grew up during the early phases of the Cold War, the erection of the Berlin Wall, and the murder of J.F. Kennedy. While the Swedish group came of age at the peak of the social engineering of the welfare state and the 'People's Home',[2] the Estonian group grew up during the Soviet occupation.

The second focus group consisted of people born in the early 1960s (1959–1966). This generation had their formative years during the later phases of the Cold War and the arms race, and ultimately the early phase of perestroika under Mikhail Gorbachev. They were in their mid-twenties when Olof Palme was murdered. This was the pre-digital era, but this generation experienced the arrival of cassette tape recorders, video and the CD record during their formative years. Most of them had children, who were in their teens or early twenties (that is, in their formative years). They were all working and had no grandchildren yet.

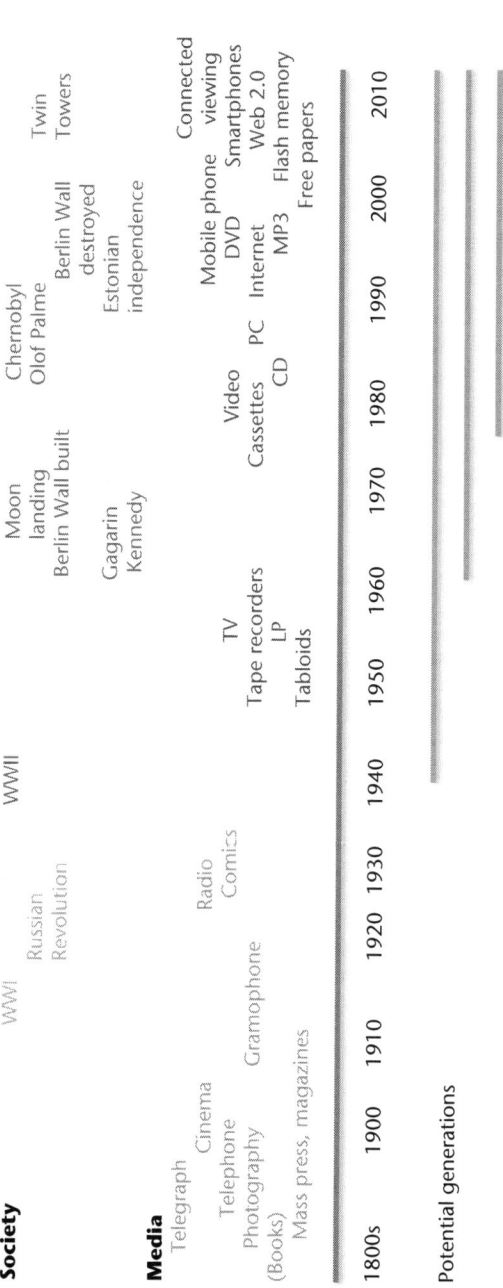

FIGURE 4.1 'Objective' media landscape 180Cs to the present, and the trajectory through it of four generations. Based on media developments in Sweden and Estonia

The members of the third focus group were born in the late 1970s (1976–1980). Tape recorders, video and CD records and the portable Walkman had always been there for them, and they saw the introduction of free daily newspapers (e.g. *Metro*), the mobile phone, DVDs, MP3s and computers during their formative years. Some were still studying, while others were working. Most of them did not have children. They were in their early teens at the time of the fall of the Berlin Wall, and at the time of Estonian independence, and had their formative years shortly afterwards.

The members of the fourth focus group were born in the early 1990s (1990–1995). They were all in their formative years at the time of the interview. The media landscape they were born into was more diverse than it had been for any of the older generational groups, although they also saw new media technologies such as the smartphone, the interactive web, music streaming services and connected viewing being introduced. They were all studying, most of them in high school (gymnasium) but some in early undergraduate studies. None of them had children. Most of them were still living with their parents.

In the next section the groups will be described and contextualised, especially in relation to their location in the media landscapes of Sweden and Estonia. Next, the chapter will analyse the ways in which these cohorts subjectively perceive of this landscape. Based on these perceptions, this chapter will first deal with cross-cultural similarities and differences in order to then discuss inter-generational relations.

Subjective generational media landscapes

The oldest generational group has travelled fifty years longer through the media landscape compared to the youngest group, and over the course of the years has seen it shift in character quite dramatically. Thus, they have fifty years longer first-hand experience of historical events, although these experiences also vary, depending on the geopolitical location in which they were encountered. That is, the fall of the Berlin Wall has had a global impact, but its meaning is supposedly different depending on whether you were living in Sweden or Estonia at the time.

Methodologically, an initial supposition was that the focus group situation, and the ways the focus groups were prompted in the interview situation, would reveal common experiences based on remembrances among the interviewees. It was expected that some of these common memories would produce a certain kind of nostalgia in relation to past experiences. All interviews started with the same prompting questions: 'Which media did you have in your home as a child?' and, 'Can you tell us about your earliest media memories?' It was presupposed that the older generation would be the one that would be more nostalgic in relation to their media memories, regarding the media landscape both as technological structure (the media technologies and gadgets they had experienced) and as symbolic environment (the texts, discourses around artists, etc.). It is reasonable to assume that this affection towards the media of one's youth gradually developed as the generation in question grew older: a kind of age component that was expected to have an impact on the generational experience and result in a process of 'generationing'

(Siibak & Vittadini 2012). It was also expected that this would be activated by the focus group situation.

While nostalgia and generationing will be discussed in more detail in the next chapter, this chapter will be devoted to an account of the different kinds of experiences of Swedish and Estonian media users to underline the spatial component in the generational identity. In order to do this, the next section will account for the media landscapes and events as experienced by the four generational pairs, since they have experienced the arrival of several new media technologies and witnessed many shifts in genre and content over the years, but in different historical contexts. The focus will first be on the cross-cultural comparison, and the inter-generational relations will be dealt with in the subsequent section.

Quite naturally, subjective media landscapes are founded on individual experiences, and are related to the specific personal context of each individual. However, each individual experience is also part of a wider pattern of experiences that are individual, yet similar to those of many others sharing the same location in the historical process. From a generational point of view it is the experiences that bind people together, the commonly developed 'media grammar' (Gumpert & Cathcart 1985), or 'generational semantics' (Colombo 2011) that are the most interesting. This chapter is, therefore, more closely focused on what features connect people and bring them together, and how such common features appear in the different interview situations.

Methodologically, this means identifying which parts of the media landscapes that have had lasting influences on the generational cohorts, and in which way remembrances are triggered when people born around the same time come together. Quite naturally, it is impossible to grasp these features in their totality because what comes up in a focus group discussion is to a certain extent dictated by which people are present (and each of their individual experiences), which societal events are on the agenda at the time of the interview, and – of course – how the moderator of the interview interacts with the interviewees.

Having stated that, the 'objective' media landscape outlined in Figure 4.1 was reflected in the focus group interviews, although emphasis was put on certain features of the landscape (rather than others). This means that one can construct a 'subjective' media landscape consisting of the media technologies and content that were mentioned and discussed during each focus group interview. This landscape is subjective in the sense that it would reflect the landscape as composed in the specific social interaction of the interviewing researcher and the interviewed individuals in the group. Again, it is important to emphasise the subjective nature of this landscape composition, as it is produced in social interaction, and need not necessarily have been represented in the same way even by the same people, were the interview to have occurred a month later, or if the group had consisted of a different combination of people. It is also subjective in the sense that it has to be lived and experienced first-hand.

The rest of this chapter will account for these subjectively experienced media landscapes. First, the four Estonian and Swedish cohorts will be accounted for pairwise, to illustrate some of the transnational experiences they share, but also to point to the geo-politically specific experiences. Thus, the culturally specific experiences will reveal and pave the way for a later discussion on the possibility of there being global experiences. Second, this chapter will analyse the intergenerational relations between the different generations. This section will focus on the specific generationing process and the formation of a collectively shared, intragenerational consciousness.

Cross-cultural comparisons: Swedish and Estonian generational landscapes

As already described, there are many similarities between the two countries, especially regarding *when* technology was introduced and established. Although the spread and domestication of technology was uneven, both between countries and within their different regions, there was an awareness of the existence of technology. Television, for example, came later to the north of Sweden compared to the big cities, but those who lived in the north of Sweden were highly aware of the fact that other Swedish citizens could watch television. This means that the oldest group of respondents, who were born during the Second World War and had their formative years in the late 1950s and early 1960s, were born into a media landscape where radio, newspapers, music media, literature, cinema, photography and telephones were already present, in the sense that they had been invented and introduced to the populations in the two countries. They saw the arrival of television during their formative years, when their media grammar was supposedly formed and established, and they were also introduced to media such as LP records and tape recorders. In that sense, these media technologies could have been expected to be natural components in the everyday life of the respondents.

The early 1940s generation

The generation born during the Second World War had their formative years in the late 1950s and the beginning of the 1960s. However, they had clear memories of the media uses that preceded their formative years, represented by both media technologies and content. The accounts of these memories make up a 'subjective' media landscape, contextualised by some very disruptive societal events that have also formed their generational experience.

In Figure 4.2, we can see the subjective media landscape of the Swedish focus group born in the early 1940s. In this figure the media phenomena that they mention are marked out, as are some news events of international magnitude, such as the Kennedy assassination in 1963, the murder of Swedish Prime Minister Olof Palme in 1985, and the attack on the World Trade Center's Twin Towers in New York in 2001. We can also see that, when prompted on what media they remember from their youth, they mention television (introduced in Sweden in the late 1950s), Radio Nord and Radio Luxembourg, both popular alternatives to the Swedish

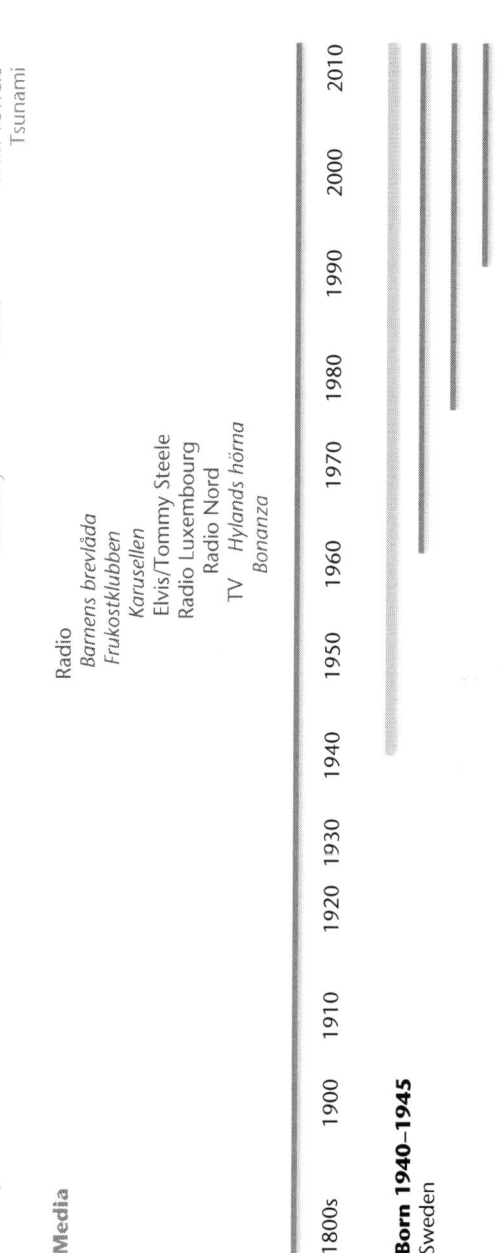

FIGURE 4.2 The 'subjective' media landscape of the Swedish early-1940s generation focus group

public service radio SR. Radio Luxembourg is well known for its international penetration, and was broadcast 1933–1939 (which naturally cannot be recalled by the focus group) and 1946–1992 (Crisell 1997). Radio Nord was a 'pirate' radio channel, broadcast from M/S Bon Jour, anchored in international waters outside Stockholm, beginning in March 1961 and broadcasting for a year, launching itself as 'Swedish commercial radio' and in clear opposition to SR (and the official media channel of Sweden). Its content was primarily popular music, which resulted in the launch of popular music on SR just a few months later (see Forsman 2010).

Much of the content on Radio Nord and Radio Luxembourg was international popular music, for example, internationally famous artists such as Tommy Steele and Elvis Presley. These artists are accordingly remembered by the informants. Both Elvis and Steele had their specific fan followings in Sweden, which is also remembered by the participants in the focus group. When it comes to television, some of the hugely popular phenomena at the time are mentioned, such as the Western series *Bonanza* (broadcast as *Bröderna Cartwright* in Sweden) and the hugely popular Saturday evening entertainment show *Hylands hörna*, led by legendary radio and television host Lennart Hyland, first in radio from 1961–1962, and then on television 1962–1983. Hyland had also hosted the popular radio show *Karusellen* (1951–1954), from which many features were imported to *Hylands hörna*.

Another programme mentioned is *Barnens brevlåda* (in translation, 'The Children's Mailbox'), a radio programme for children, broadcast 1925–1972, for its duration led by legendary radio host Sven Jerring. Another common experience was listening to *Frukostklubben*, broadcast on Saturday mornings and for children to listen to before leaving for school (as one did on Saturdays in Sweden until 1968). *Frukostklubben* was a morning show broadcast between 1946–1949, and after a few years' break between 1955–1978. It was most likely the earlier period in which the respondents listened (as they had finished school by 1955).

This landscape can be contrasted with the media landscape of the corresponding Estonian generation, as represented by the Estonian focus group of interviewees born 1939–1946. In Figure 4.3 we can see that the societal events mentioned differ from those referred to by their Swedish coevals, and are more connected to the respondents' geopolitical and cultural position in Soviet Estonia. Rather than the moon landing, it is the memory of Soviet astronaut Yuri Gagarin, the first man to travel in space, in May 1961 that comes to mind. Memories of wartime are also clearly present, with some informants giving accounts of time spent in Siberia.

When it comes to the media, the radio has a very prominent position. There are, however, very few references to programmes or content on the radio – the only radio content referred to is *Voice of America* (broadcast since 1942). The accounts are more about the radio as a technology or device. The significance of radio as a technology is clearly enhanced by the fact that the authorities confiscated radio transmitters during and shortly after the war. People had to hide them away if they were to keep them, and several of the respondents describe this.

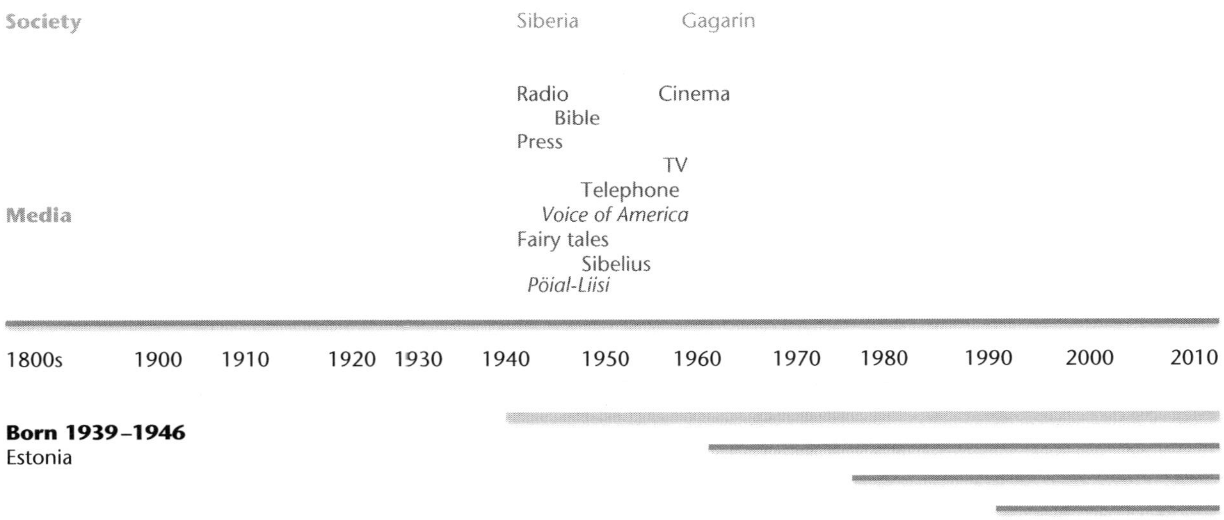

Society

Siberia   Gagarin

Cinema

Media

Radio
Bible
Press
TV
Telephone
Voice of America
Fairy tales
Sibelius
Pöial-Liisi

1800s   1900   1910   1920   1930   1940   1950   1960   1970   1980   1990   2000   2010

Born 1939–1946
Estonia

FIGURE 4.3   The 'subjective' media landscape of the Estonian early-1940s generation focus group

Another medium emphasised by the Estonian respondents born in the early 1940s is the telephone. Telephone access was scarce during and after the war, and, in a similar way to radio, its use was collective and the technology shared. Two of the Swedish respondents in the same generation also had no telephone at home during their first years, and can vividly recall the sense of achievement when they got one in the early 1950s. Both radio and telephone were thus 'objectively' existing technologies in the media landscape at the time, but were not available in the homes of some of the respondents, and it is obvious that this lack makes the arrival of the technology in the home so much more memorable.

In the Estonian focus group of the early 1940s generation, memories of children's books are also recounted. One of the respondents mentions receiving *Pöial-Liisi* (H.C. Andersen's *Thumbelina*) as a present from her aunt when she was four years old and in hospital for diphtheria. Another respondent tells how her interest in reading began with *Tsaari Kuller* (original *Michel Strogoff*, 1876, and published in English as *Michael Strogoff: The Courier of the Czar*) by Jules Verne, which she read when visiting her aunt. The old edition with its Gothic letters, which were hard to read, is still in her memory.

It was of course highly expected that the Second World War would cast different shadows on the Swedish and Estonian respondents. The media, especially radio, are clearly related to wartime, especially for the Estonian respondents, and the sensitive issue of having access to radio appears in several of the respondents' accounts. If the radio is connected to the war and the political situation for the Estonian respondents, it is more connected to popular music and youth culture for their Swedish counterparts. Both groups mention influences from abroad, but whereas the Estonian respondents mention classical music and Sibelius, transmitted from stations in Finland, the Swedish respondents report on the influx of Anglo-American popular music via Radio Luxembourg and Swedish pirate radio stations.

The Estonian respondents also give accounts of formative moments that took place in their very early childhood years through traditional children's fairy tales (H.C. Andersen) and adventure novels typical of the youth period (Jules Verne). Children's books and fairy tales are absent from the accounts of the Swedish members of the early 1940s generation, and literature is only mentioned when they describe their formative years. It is also evident that the Estonian respondents think of the radio in terms of a device, something that had to be hidden during and after the war since it could possibly connect to the world outside Soviet Estonia. Radio was a means to reach outside in Sweden as well, but rather to the international cultural world beyond the country's media landscape, where one could listen to the international pop music that – at least at first – could not be accessed through Swedish Radio.

The early 1960s generation

The generation born in the early 1960s was born into an 'objective' media landscape where not only radio, telephone, the press and the cinema were already present, but where television also existed, even if some families did not yet have access to it in their homes. Their formative years occurred in the second half of the 1970s and the 1980s, at the height of the Cold War, and in the shadow of the nuclear 'balance of terror'. The arms race and the political tensions between the First and Second Worlds are, however, absent from both the Swedish and Estonian interviews, and form more of a general background to other, more personal, stories (of course, dictated by the interview setup).

As illustrated in Figure 4.4, the Swedish respondents who were born in the early 1960s have clear memories of the moon landing (even if some also reflect on whether their experience is from a later date: that is, they might not have seen the landing when it occurred but rather in reruns afterwards). Like the Swedish 1940s generation, they have strong memories of the murder of Olof Palme in 1985. They also have clear memories of sports events, foremost the international success in tennis of Björn Borg, who had his most successful period between 1974 and 1981, and slalom skier Ingemar Stenmark, whose career also peaked in the late 1970s and early 1980s.

It is obvious from the interviews that television was the most important medium for them when they were very young – that is before the age of ten. There is one exception in the group who holds radio as more important, since she grew up in Liberia, Africa, and did not have access to television. However, not many children's programmes are mentioned, but rather sports events (Borg, Stenmark, World Soccer championships, etc.), events that relate more to the respondents' formative years than to their childhood.

A common discussion in the 1960s focus group was comics (*MAD, Fantomen, Agent X9*) (cf. Aroldi & Ponte [2012] on a similar attraction to comics in Italy among respondents born roughly at the same time). A special feature related to the comic magazines was the opportunity to find pen pals through them. This is also contrasted by the respondents in reference to younger generations, who supposedly do not write traditional letters but rather communicate via e-mail and social networking sites. Another prominent feature was the introduction of the cassette tape recorder, which allowed you to produce mix tape recordings of your favourite songs from the radio.

In the group discussion the respondents commented on the intangible character of contemporary, digital media. In several instances there was an emphasis on the materiality of cassette tapes, LP records – especially their album covers – and the tangibility and 'rustly' sound of the printed newspaper.

The first media memories of this Estonian generation are related to children's radio and television shows, when the respondents were around four to five years old (see Figure 4.5). They also have a discussion about how well they remember the details of these shows: the opening music, the main characters, and so on, of television shows such as *Telepoiss* (The TV Boy, 1962–)[3] and the puppet show *Tipp ja Täpp* (1969–).[4] The television experiences differ depending on whether the respondent was brought up in Tallinn or another part of Estonia. In Tallinn it was possible to tune into Finnish television (YLE), and thus have access to Western television programmes.[5] Many built their own television receivers, a phenomenon that

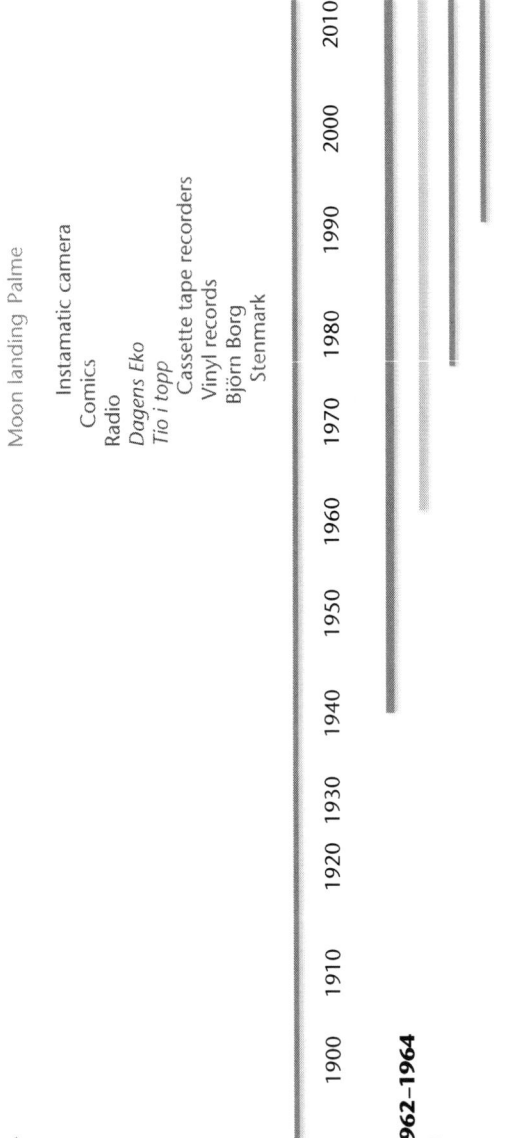

FIGURE 4.4 The 'subjective' media landscape of the Swedish early-1960s generation focus group

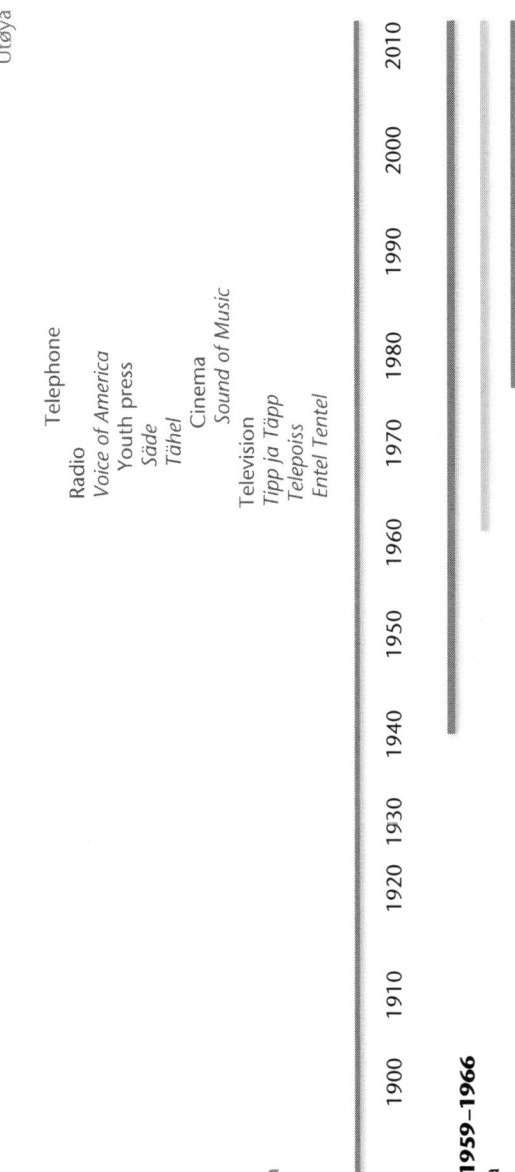

FIGURE 4.5 The 'subjective' media landscape of the Estonian early–1960s generation focus group

is vividly recalled in the (fictional) film *Disco and Atomic War* (2009, original *Disko ja tuumasõda*), which has been held to be characteristic of this specific generation:

> A story about growing up in the Soviet Union. The film tells the story of a strange kind of information war, where a totalitarian regime stands face to face with the heroes of popular culture. And loses. It was a time when it was possible for erotic film star Emmanuelle to bring down the Red Army and MacGyver to outdo an entire school administration. It is a film about our generation, who were unknowingly brought to the front line of the Cold War. Western popular culture had an incomparable role shaping Soviet children's world views in those days. Finnish television was a window to a world of dreams that the authorities could not block in any way. Though Finnish channels were banned, many households found some way to access the forbidden fruit.
>
> *(imdb.com, plot summary)*[6]

Also mentioned in the interview are many youth newspapers and magazines, for example *Säde* (The Spark), launched in 1946 and published twice a week for schoolchildren, and the extremely popular children's journal *Täheke* (The Little Star), published from 1960 and at the peak of its popularity in the 1980s with a print run of 80,000 copies.[7]

In the post-war years, cinema increasingly became a phenomenon related to youth. While television became the medium for small children and parents, youth socialised around the cinema – in Sweden, Estonia and elsewhere in the world (cf. Doherty 1988). However, for this Estonian generation, cinema carried a very special significance. During the formative years of this group, several new cinemas were built in Tallinn (and in other parts of the country), where you could occasionally watch foreign, Western films. *The Sound of Music* (1965) is mentioned by several informants, and seems to have been shown in theatres in Tallinn around the mid-1970s, but French comedies (Louis de Funes) and Indian films are also mentioned. This was perceived as a sensational break with the propaganda films of earlier periods.

Another phenomenon with no counterpart for the corresponding Swedish generation was the *Plaadimägi* (roughly: the record hill) market, which took place on Sundays on the Harju hill in the centre of Tallinn throughout the 1970s and 1980s. This is where Western pop music records were traded and swapped, and a Beatles record could cost as much as half a month's salary. Although it was tempting for the young Estonians to go there to take part in this 'forbidden' market, those who did not live in Tallinn had restricted opportunities to attend each weekend. Being part of the Plaadimägi market was considered somewhat rebellious, and had a kind of subcultural air to it.

A further difference between Sweden and Estonia was that comics were not a part of the 'objective' media landscape in Estonia, whereas they were in Sweden. As Piermarco Aroldi and Cristina Ponte (2012) show in a generational analysis also involving people born around 1960, comics were an important new medium for those growing up in the 1960s and 1970s, and in this sense the 'objective' media landscape of Western Europe seems to have provided other media, with other opportunity structures. The popular music present in Western Europe, which was also significant for the 1960s generation, with mix tapes that could circulate among friends and thus be the focus of social meetings within the generation, had its corresponding feature in the Plaadimägi market for popular music.

For these reasons, it is important to acknowledge the differences between the 'objective' media landscapes of Sweden and Estonia. For all our generations, the press, weekly magazines, cinema and radio were already there as media. Television arrived almost at the same time in both countries technologically, although it is obvious from the interviews that not everyone had access in their own homes before the 1970s, whereas in Sweden 90 per cent already had access in 1963 (Findahl 2013: 19). The landline telephone, however, was not as widespread in Estonia as in Sweden. The mobile phone arrived around the same time in the two countries, and although penetration initially was slightly slower in Estonia, it quite soon reached the same level as in Sweden (that is, around 95 per cent, cf. Bolin 2010: 61). However, while most of the media appeared simultaneously, the content of the mass media differed considerably, especially for the Estonian respondents before independence.

The late 1970s generation

Those who were born in the late 1970s grew up in a landscape where television, tape recorders, video and CD records and the portable Walkman was a natural given. This cohort saw the introduction of free daily newspapers (e.g. *Metro*), the mobile phone, DVDs, MP3s and computers during their formative years. They were on the brink of their teenage years when the Berlin Wall fell in November 1989, and at the time of Estonian independence in 1991, and were at the peak of their formative years shortly afterwards.

The first media memories of the Swedish focus group respondents born towards the end of the 1970s are focused on popular music in radio and television – when Sweden won the Eurovision Song Contest of 1984, or the Saturday afternoon music list *Trackslistan*, where the most popular music of the time was played (Figure 4.6). The broadcasting of *Trackslistan* was also an event where the informants recorded mix-tapes on cassette, typical for the time. Other common memories that appear are children's television programmes, most notably the highly popular pedagogic series *Fem myror är fler än fyra elefanter* (Five ants are more than four elephants), originally broadcast 1973–1974, and with a Christmas special in 1977 (the annual Christmas calendar that is broadcast on each day for the month before Christmas). However, the memories of this programme must stem from the continuous reruns of this immensely popular series (which is still broadcast today).

The news event of the murder of Swedish Prime Minister Olof Palme in February 1986 is vividly remembered, for some to the point of recalling what they were doing and where they were when the news arrived on the radio, and on television.

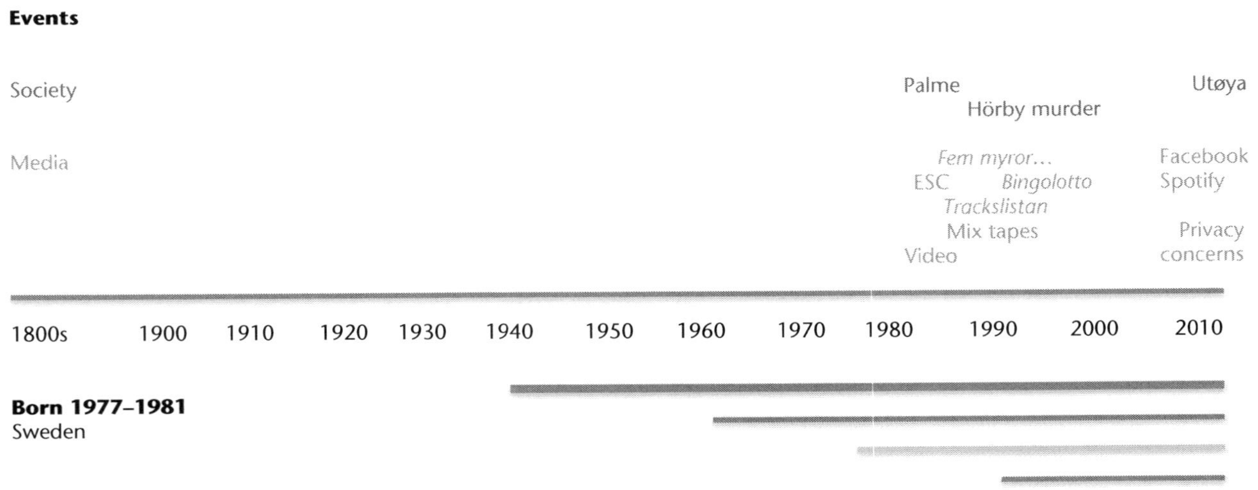

Events

Society

Media

| 1800s | 1900 | 1910 | 1920 | 1930 | 1940 | 1950 | 1960 | 1970 | 1980 | 1990 | 2000 | 2010 |

Society: Palme · Hörby murder · Utøya

Media: *Fem myror...* · *Bingolotto* · ESC · *Trackslistan* · Mix tapes · Video · Facebook · Spotify · Privacy concerns

Born 1977–1981
Sweden

FIGURE 4.6 The 'subjective' media landscape of the Swedish late-1970s generation focus group

Some received the news on radio the night that the murder occurred, a Friday evening, while others discovered the news on breakfast television the next morning. The focus group respondents were very young at this point in time – between the ages of five or six and nine, depending on if they were born early or late in the year – but it is evident that the memory, naturally also enforced by the reaction to the news of their parents, has had a lasting impact. One informant exclaimed that 'I was going to watch *Good Morning, Sweden* in the morning, but there was nothing. It was news instead, so I ran to wake up mum and dad. I realised that it was something big'. The general seriousness of the tone of the news has imprinted this moment in the young person in a way that forms the experience not only of news, but also marks out this moment in Swedish contemporary history, similarly to how other murders of state heads and prominent figures have been imprinted in the minds of audiences all over the world. It is quite clear that despite being very young at that moment, and maybe having very vague ideas of who Olof Palme was, the news broadcast itself had the ability to leave such deep imprints on the group.

Another murder was discussed in the group, a particularly gruesome sexual murder of a 10-year-old girl in the village of Hörby in 1989. This story, however, was featured in the news for a long time (the actual murderer was only found sixteen years later, in 2005). Therefore, the memories and the discussion of this focus less on the actual moment at which one received the news, and more on the unfolding of the event, and of the fact that the abducted girl was in the same age bracket as the informants. Still, it is a news story that most in the group seem familiar with.

Interestingly enough, this focus group share more memories of their childhood, than from formative years. Other features discussed as common experiences are more related to the present.

The Estonian focus group of this potential generation also becomes more engaged when topics concerning childhood memories are discussed (Figure 4.7). Again, and similar to the Swedish group, they have vivid memories not only of children's television but also of news programmes, especially the programme *Vremja*: from 1968 the main news programme broadcast by the USSR's Central Television.

All focus group respondents remember *Vremja*, since it cut through the television schedule, irrespective of what was on (and for the respondents, it was at this time mainly the children's programmes). The memories of *Vremja* are, however, negative, since the programme was in Russian, and, as one interviewee says, since 'children didn't understand Russian, *Vremja* seemed like such a pointless programme'.

A major societal event that was noted in the focus group was the death of Leonid Brezhnev in 1982, mainly by two (of the five) interviewees who were five and six years old at the time (the three others were only two years old). However, their memories clearly seem to be incorporated into family history, where it is repeated as a significant moment:

Ivan: When Brezhnev died, there was... mourning! And...

Andres: A day off school!

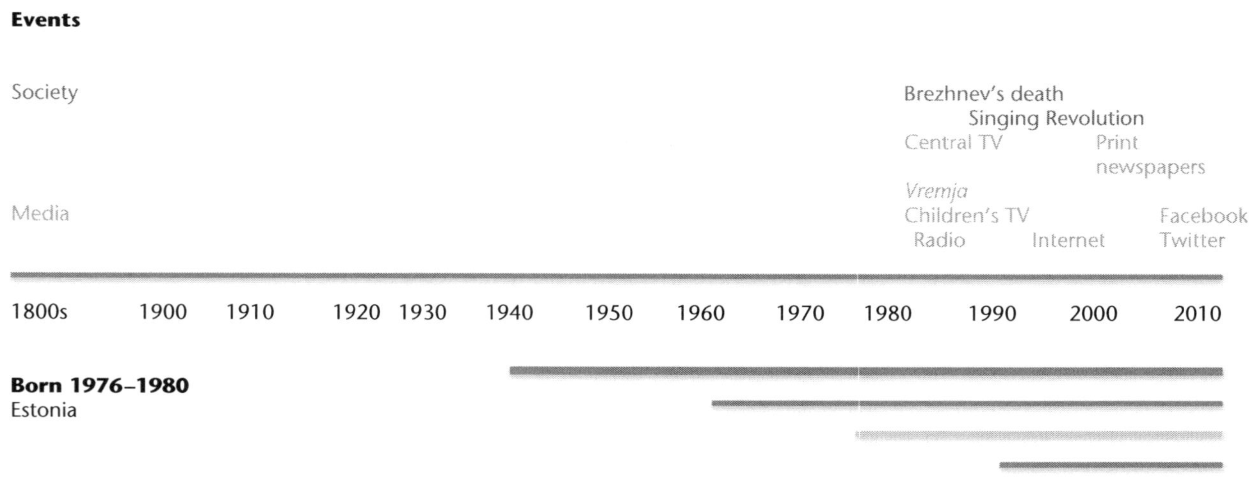

Events

Society

Brezhnev's death
Singing Revolution
Central TV   Print
                    newspapers

Media

Vremja   Facebook
Children's TV   Twitter
Radio   Internet

1800s 1900 1910 1920 1930 1940 1950 1960 1970 1980 1990 2000 2010

Born 1976–1980
Estonia

FIGURE 4.7 The 'subjective' media landscape of the Estonian late-1970s generation focus group

Ivan: I don't know... I didn't go to school yet, but... there were no kids' shows on TV for several days. My mum has told me that I and my sister had said that well... we'd had enough of mourning and we wanted kids' TV shows.

This is obviously a memory enforced through repeated retelling in the family ('mum has told me...'). Nonetheless, it is an event that engages not only Ivan, but also Andres, but in hindsight, thirty years after the event. What their actual reactions at the time were, we cannot know, but this event has stood out as a marker in time that involves significant points in political history, framed by the media context and related to the everyday life of watching children's television programmes that were regularly interrupted by Russian-language news. The memory has been moulded in the generationing process (Siibak & Vittadini 2012), and adjusted to the generational consciousness.

A more abrupt shift occurred in the Estonian media landscape was the Singing Revolution, the peaceful protests in the form of mass singing demonstrations, which began in the late 1980s and led to Estonian independence in 1991. The citizens gathered in choirs to sing national hymns, and this is also something that the Estonian focus group interviewees remember and remark on in several instances during the interview. The interviewees also talk about how the media system changed, how 'television became especially important', and how the radio content changed. The account is not entirely uncritical, and the respondents also talk about the lack of depth in online journalism and the advantages of print newspapers with longer, feature articles.

The respondents in this generational focus group were obviously brought up during the shift from print media to online media, which is revealed by their quite ambivalent relation to these two different publishing forms. They all read online news, but they also all have vivid memories of newspapers, and quite a few of them at the time of being interviewed read newspapers and magazines on paper, mixed with their online reading. They relatively frequently refer to media memories connected to their parents or grandparents, and it is obvious that some of their opinions are formed by previous media grammars, inherited from the previous generations.

The early 1990s generation

The youngest of the interviewed generational cohorts were all in their formative years at the time of the interview, being in high school or early undergraduate studies. They were born into a much more pluralistic media landscape compared to any of the older generation cohorts, and grew up in a continuously changing media environment with new media such as the smartphone, the interactive web (including social networking and geo-local media), music streaming services and connected viewing being introduced. Importantly, they had not yet formed individual households, and were still living with their parents.

The Swedish interviewees share common memories of video as a medium, with children's films (Figure 4.8). Also *Björnes magasin*, the daily block of children's

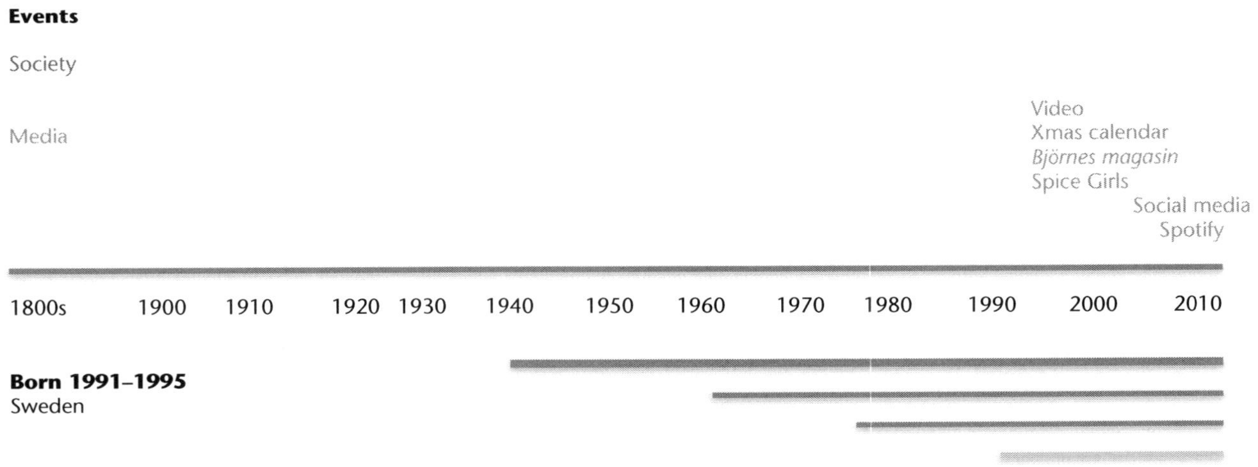

Events

Society

Media

| | 1800s | 1900 | 1910 | 1920 | 1930 | 1940 | 1950 | 1960 | 1970 | 1980 | 1990 | 2000 | 2010 |

Video
Xmas calendar
Björnes magasin
Spice Girls
Social media
Spotify

Born 1991–1995
Sweden

FIGURE 4.8 The 'subjective' media landscape of the Swedish early–1990s generation focus group

programmes on public service Swedish Television is remembered vividly by all in the focus group. This is by no means strange, since these were the early days of the plural Swedish media landscape that up until around 1990 had been dominated by public service television. That the interviewees also remember the Christmas calendar that is broadcast each year from the 1 December until Christmas Eve is not strange either, since basically all Swedish children do. Since the theme of the Christmas calendar changes for each year, it would be more formative had the group as a whole focused on one of these, but that was not the case. The same goes for *Björnes magasin*, which is a block of programmes with short animated films, knitted together by the bear Björne as the studio host who also sometimes has guests in the studio, reads viewers' letters, and so on. All in all, one can say that while this group do have shared experiences and can describe media technologies that they have in common, or contemporary pop stars such as the Spice Girls, they do not become as engaged as did the older cohorts interviewed.

If we turn to the Estonian interviewees, the same goes for them. They were all born in independent Estonia, and have no first-hand memories of the Soviet times (although they naturally get stories from parents and other older socialising agents). Figure 4.9 shows the media and contents mentioned by the informants during the interview. The interviewees have memories of radio (Vikerraadio), LP records, children's television and when they received their first computer. The memories are often connected to family situations. They are, however, very individual and do not spark off a common engagement in the focus group situation. It is obvious that those common experiences that there are have not triggered any generational commonality that makes the respondents think of themselves in terms of a generation.

Cross-cultural differences in the Estonian and Swedish generational landscapes

Against the background of the above descriptions of the generational pairs, we can now make some more general comments on the cross-cultural differences. Again, there are many similarities between the two countries, especially when it comes to when technology was introduced and established. And although the spread and domestication of technology was uneven, both between countries and within different regions within them, there was an awareness of the existence of technology. Television, for example, came later to the north of Sweden compared to when it arrived in the big cities. However, those who lived in the north of Sweden were highly aware of the fact that other Swedish citizens could watch, and hence television was present in the national imagination – also for those who actually had no access, or could only see it in the homes of friends, or at special publicly arranged occasions (cf. Höijer 1998: 158ff). This means that the oldest group of respondents, born during the Second World War and who had their formative years in the late-1950s and early-1960s, were born into a media landscape where radio, newspapers, music media, literature, cinema, photography and telephones were already present, in the sense that they had been invented and introduced to the populations in the

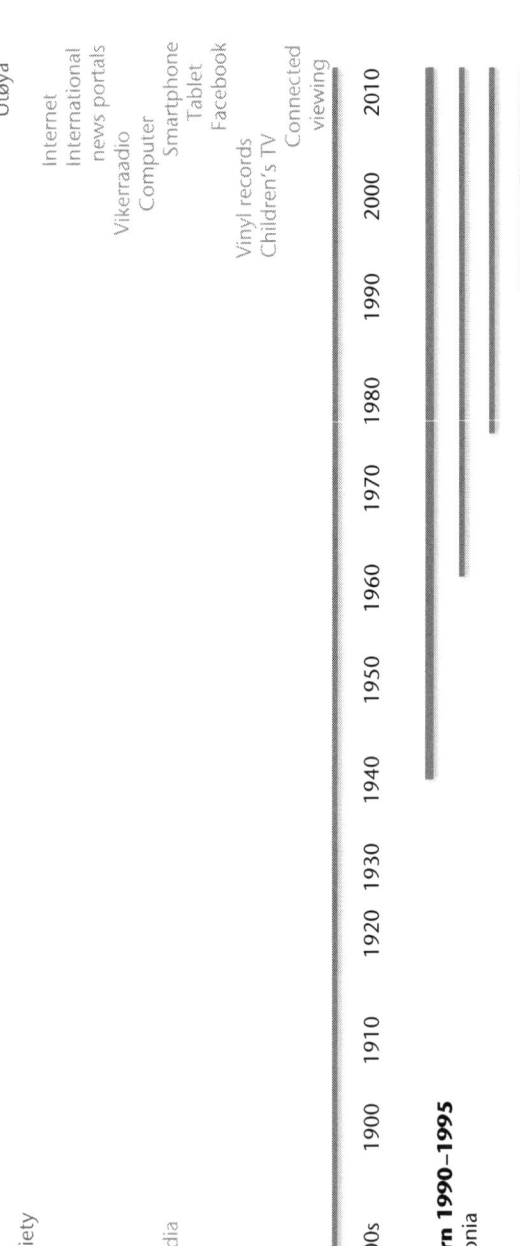

Society

Utøya

Internet
International
news portals
Vikerraadio
Computer
Smartphone
Tablet
Facebook
Vinyl records
Children's TV
Connected
viewing

Media

1800s   1900   1910   1920   1930   1940   1950   1960   1970   1980   1990   2000   2010

Born 1990–1995
Estonia

FIGURE 4.9 The 'subjective' media landscape of the Estonian early-1990s generation focus group

two countries. They saw the arrival of television during their formative years, when their media grammar was supposedly formed and established, and they were also introduced to media such as LP and EP records, and tape recorders. In that sense, these media technologies could have been expected to be natural components in the everyday life of the respondents.

However, the generations born during the war were not only confronted with new media technologies but they also faced a number of dramatic societal events. There is, however, a stark arrhythmia produced by the meeting of the geo-social (or geo-political) and the technological rhythms. This is maybe most obvious when it comes to the telephone – a technology that had long since been invented and established in both countries. As discussed in the previous chapter, the telephone was an already domesticated medium in Sweden in the post-war period, whereas in Estonia it was not. The telephone system was also restricted and controlled in a way that it was not in Sweden, with an absence of telephone directories, and tight control of who had access in the homes. In the words of one focus group member: 'there was an enormous waiting list' if one wanted to have a phone. As Lars Kleberg (2012: 19) has pointed out, the limited circulation of telephone directories in the Soviet Union, and the constant threat of being wiretapped, deprived citizens of the means to communicate with one another, and was in the Stalinist era introduced as a consciously utilised political means for avoiding counter-revolution and conspiracy (cf. Boettiger 1977).

It should also come as no surprise that the content of the media varies between the two national contexts, and particularly during the Soviet times. This is especially so when it comes to the traditional mass media, where the content in Soviet Estonia was heavily controlled by the authorities. The press, for example, meant something entirely different in the two national settings: to Estonians the press connoted propaganda and represented the official party line (see, e.g. Lauk 1999), whereas for the Swedish respondents it represented an adult medium that their parents – primarily the fathers – engaged in, echoing results from other Western countries (cf. Volkmer 2006b: 258f). Popular music was also heavily controlled in the Estonian setting, which is exemplified by the Plaadimägi market example, where Western music signified freedom and for a person to engage in appreciation of Western music was seen as somewhat rebellious in a way that it was not in Sweden – at least not in the same way.

There are some notable thematic similarities related to news events, for example related to the space race between Soviet Union and United States. However, thematic similarity does not equal identical approaches to the space race, and in fact one can see that the emphasis is very different and can be attributed to the national context in which reception took place. Thus, when Swedish respondents emphasised the moon landing of Apollo 11, Estonian respondents talked about Gagarin. Both these events indicate the importance of the space race, but from different communicative horizons. This is not really grounded in a lack of reporting: while Gagarin's space travel was widely reported internationally, including in the Swedish press (Åker 2015) and television (Lundgren 2012), this event does not seem to have stuck in the minds of the Swedish respondents, whereas the moon landing has – as it has for several informants in Höijer's (1998: 204) study of media memories. There is thus an emphasis on the space race in both of the countries, but with characteristic differences in the way in which it was reported on in the mass media in each national setting (cf. Jirák 2006: 64).

There is also a strong emphasis on the radio medium in many of the focus groups, irrespective of birth cohort. However, whereas one could presume that this similarity would produce a similarity in responses, this is not really the case. Although radio was considered the most significant medium especially among the older groups of respondents, the stories they tell around radio differ considerably. On the one hand, to the Swedes the radio was a symbol of the world outside, where international radio stations for light entertainment music such as Radio Luxembourg or Radio Hilversum were mentioned (cf. Höijer 1998: 116f). On the other hand, it meant specific programming directed towards children and young people, for example the programme *Barnens brevlåda* (The Children's Letterbox), which was immensely popular among children from its start in 1925 and onwards for several decades until it stopped in 1972 (Höijer 1998: 72ff and 133f). To Estonian respondents, however, radio signifies something completely different, as radio receivers were forbidden during the Soviet times:

> *Urve*: I got my own radio in 1967. We once had a radio in the country, but these were confiscated during the war.
>
> *Mare*: That's why ours was hidden.
>
> *Interviewer*: But why? To prevent people from getting information or what was the reason?
>
> *Maido*: Yes.
>
> *Mare*: Russians confiscated them elsewhere too.
>
> *Urve*: They were taken away.
>
> *Mare*: We had both of ours hidden. Village men came and took them.
>
> *Urve*: Ours was taken away too. My mother said it was a beautiful and expensive German radio.
>
> *(Estonian focus group, born 1939–1945)*

As the quote shows, radio was more thought of in terms of the technology and its status as a forbidden medium, one that had to be used secretly if at all. The materiality of the medium is further enforced by Urve's comment on the actual design components and the apparent value of the object. Such comments are absent in the Swedish interviews.

In summary, from the cross-cultural analysis we can learn that it is important to situate generation not only in the historical, temporal location but also in specific geo-cultural and geo-political locations. One cannot presume that just because the media technologies are the same in two national contexts, media users will relate in the same way to them. Generational experience is clearly culturally specific to the specific location in which experience takes place.

Intergenerational differences in Sweden and Estonia

The previous sub-section has discussed the cross-cultural differences and similarities in the material. We shall now turn to the intergenerational relations and analyse how generations relate to both older and younger generations: thus we will try to get to the rhythms produced by generational exchanges. Two types of relations will be discussed: indirect and direct intergenerational relations.

Indirect intergenerational relations are those relations that are not explicitly addressed by the respondents in interviews, but that are revealed in the different media technologies and content that respondents describe, or emphasise in the interview situation. This means that respondents do not explicitly reflect on their media preferences by way of relating them to other generations but more that the intergenerational relations appear in the analysis, produced as a difference by the researcher. One example of this can be the emphasis that the generational groups born in the early 1940s made on the radio medium: an emphasis that distinguishes them from most other groups of interviewees. Thus one might say that the individuals in these interview groups have formed a generation through their shared relation to the radio medium.

This is not exactly the same generational labelling as that which is produced by the quantitative data that most generation analysts rely on, which is merely generation as location (that is, not as actuality). Indirect generational relations are not only defined by common habits but are also expressed in the vivid engagement in the focus group discussion. For example, when one focus group member talks about a radio or television programme, a well-known societal event, or, as in the quote below, the habit of going to the cinema, and the others support and confirm the similarity in feeling.

> *Interviewer*: I mean, what kind of films did they show mostly at that time?
>
> *Aire*: Indian films.
>
> *Merike*: Yes, Indian films.
>
> *Ruth*: French comedies.
>
> *Aire*: Yes. Louis de Funes.
>
> *Toomas*: Louis de Funes, yes.
>
> *Merike*: Oktoober or Pioneer, which one was there on Viru street, where they showed one film all day and you could enter whenever you wanted?
>
> *Toomas*: Yes, yes.
>
> *Aire*: It was Pioneer.

Merike: They were both actually in that area.

Ruth: Both were there.

Aire: Yes, Pioneer. Oktoober was where they sometimes had theatrical plays.

Toomas: And there was Foorum.

Interviewer: How many films were specifically for the youth at that time? Or was it more of peeping into the adult world?

Sirje: There was no difference.

Aire: I think everyone went.

Helle: Everyone went.

Merike: Exept those prohibited, that were under 14...

Toomas: Yes, yes.

Aire: Certainly *Romeo and Juliet* had an asterisk on the title. It meant it was prohibited up to a certain age. And it was a very good film!

Merike: You put on lipstick and wore your aunt's hat and went anyway.

(Focus group Estonia, born 1959–1966)

In the focus group situation, this specific kind of engagement is revealed in the enthusiastic 'yes, yes' utterances from other members of the interview group, and the discussion about the different cinema theatres as a confirmation of the common memory of going to the cinema in these specific times (and at those specific places). In fact, one can argue that these are the very points at which generational commonality – or 'we-sense' – occur, if only for that single moment when memories are revived and the focus group attendants are revisiting their younger selves.

The focus group situation can thus be seen as part of the continuous construction of the overall grand narrative of the generation, and an indication of the generationing process. The we-sense is not always articulated explicitly, but has to be read in the interaction of the focus group participants, as in the following quote from the focus group of Estonian media users in retirement, also discussing cinema from their formative years.

Heidi: I went to the cinema a long time ago. A very long time ago. I was still a child, the cinema was far. Two kilometres from the schoolhouse, but I went...

Mare: There was a party after the film.

Heidi: Yes, a dance, a big dance.

Mare: Very much so. It was like that in Estonia. In Siberia they showed films outside, people gathered by the screen. It was the same in Estonia, when I returned there was travelling cinema in the countryside.

Interviewer: What type of films did they show? Were they feature films?

Mare: Valgus Koordis[8] and such things... Of course, also Russian films.

Interviewer: Was that considered propaganda cinema?

Urve: No, no.

Mare: It was art...

Heidi: I can't say it was propaganda, but there was always a newsreel... Stalin... those showed everything that was going on.

Mare: There were foreign films too.

Urve: We had films at school. In the daytime, those village parties, here in Tartu. They showed *The Great Waltz* and something else.[9] The films were certainly nice.

Interviewer: Were you in school then?

Urve: Yes, I was in school. It was in 1956–1957.

Mare: This was the cinema at the time. There were English films and Italian films too.

Heidi: And Indian love films.

Urve: India.

Mare: Italian, Spanish films.

Lev: German films.

Mare: There were German films.

Urve: Then we went to buy tickets straight away.

Mare: The Russian films were good too.

Urve: Yes, they were.

Mare: There were war films. And nice films too.

Urve: There was Karla Savi, who was cross with us: 'What, you will go to arrive on time?'[10]

Mare: There were also broadcast plays, Mari Möldre [famous actress] was playing...

Interviewer: Do you mean radio plays?

Mare: Yes, that's right.

Interviewer: Were they popular?

Mare: They were certainly funny.

Urve: Yes, we all heard them on the radio...

Mare: Ervin Abel [a legendary comic actor] came later, right?

Urve: Yes.

Mare: [Sulev] Nõmmik [a comic actor and film director] came later too, I think...We heard a lot of songs by [Georg] Ots [an opera singer]. The father of Georg Ots too. They played opera songs.

Urve: Yes, we knew all of these.

Mare: 'Kõik õied ma kingiksin sulle' ['All the roses I will bring to you'] and... I was sixteen, and it was my favourite song.

In the quote we can see how the generational we-sense gradually evolves in the taking turns and how the participants confirm each other's experiences. The 'we' expressed on several occasions – such as 'we all heard them on the radio' or 'we knew all of these' – is the 'we' as in 'our generation'. Even if it is very clear that it is prompted by the interview situation it is nonetheless an expression of belonging and an aspired generational commonality, waiting to become confirmed.

Direct intergenerational relations, on the other hand, are revealed by way of explicit reference to other generations than one's own: for example, through statements about 'the younger generation' or the 'parents' generation'. This does not necessarily involve the exact word 'generation', but can just as well be in the form of someone referring to his or her children by way of emphasising difference in habit or approach – a 'generational demarcation' (generationelle Abgrenzung; Hepp, Berg & Roitsch 2015: 27ff) that marks out the limits regarding other age cohorts or generations:

> *Marie*: Well, I think in fact that I am closer to my parents compared to how my own children are to me, because I had to learn the digital world as a grown up. I belonged to the analogue world in the sense that while my children learned all this as children... So, I mean, they are more of a digital generation.
>
> [...]
>
> My children never read comics much. In fact, I didn't get the sense that it was such a strong influence in their childhood as it was for me.
>
> [...]
>
> *Mats*: Well, I know because I have saved all my comic magazines, so they [the children] got quite a strong dose anyway. What was a bit disappointing was that *Agent X9* and *Fantomen*, and the others, they were in black and white, and then it wasn't much fun.
>
> *(Focus group, Sweden, born 1962–1964)*

> Our generation seems to have quite a lot of similarities in their media use. When you look at people who are 10–15 years younger, they are many times more superficial. It's another world actually.
>
> *(Focus group, Estonia, born 1976–1980)*

These quotes point to the marking of a generational belonging that differs from younger generations. By pointing to how different younger persons are, a common understanding that 'we' in the focus group have something in common that distinguishes us from younger persons is produced (in the interview situation). There is thus a specific 'we-sense' implied by the person making the statement. This we-sense is also produced in relation to older generations:

> I think the most important thing with the Internet is… er, yes, maybe not the most important but still a very central part of it is the possibility to search for information. There I can see a very big difference towards my parent generation, and some are… some are very good at Internet and Googling and so on, and others do not even know how to upload a picture on the screen, sort of.
>
> *(Focus group, Sweden, born 1962–1964)*

An interesting feature in some of the interviews is that the interviewees are reluctant to see themselves as less technologically savvy compared to younger generations, although at the same time marking distance from older generations, who are indeed seen as technologically incompetent. In the Swedish focus group of people born 1940–1945, for example, the respondents emphasised that the difference from younger people is not that big when it comes to the use of digital media, and that their less frequent use of social networking media and various applications on mobile phones and the Internet is not because of lack of competence or skills, but rather because there is no specific need to spend so much time with these media. At the same time, this group points out that there was a vast difference to their own parents, who were never capable of understanding new media such as mobile phones or television:

> *Carin:* What I remember is when my sister and I went up north to see my mother, when she had… my sister had gotten herself a mobile phone. And mum, she just couldn't understand how she could… we were in a grocery store and then my sister called her husband to ask if there was anything specific she should buy, and she said: 'but can she really talk with Kjell here in the store? Don't we have to get back home first?'. It was really difficult for her to grasp that this telephone could connect from wherever you were.
>
> *Benny:* It was the same with the telvision. Many believed that the TV signal came through the electric wall socket.
>
> *(Focus group, Sweden, born 1940–1945)*

This marking of a distance towards the parents' generation is echoed in other interviews, with younger focus group members:

> *Interviewer:* Do you sometimes watch together with siblings or parents?
>
> *Ronja:* Yes, I do. I mostly watch with my sister. But also with Daddy. I have

taught him how to connect the laptop to the TV so we can watch SVT Play on the TV.

Interviewer: OK, so you watch on a larger screen?

Ronja: Yes, and then it is like watching in the ordinary way. Then I watch with him.

(Focus group, Sweden, born 1991–1995)

In general, then, respondents point out that they are not in any way restricted when it comes to the ability of using new media technologies. In addition, the older respondents are on Facebook and other social networking media, and they strongly underline that there are no technological obstacles for them – it is merely a question of relevance, where they do not really see the point of spending so much time there.

At the same time there are several indications of a perceived distance to the parents' generation, who have not had the technological abilities needed to use new media, or never really have understood the media use of the respondents, and have thought it to be too loud, or too vulgar.

Gunvor: What I mean is, I could use it if I wanted to, but I have never really… only decided for myself that I… that it doesn't suit me. I think it takes too much time, and, then I think you become so restricted, so tied up. Dependent, yes, dependent…

Marianne: Yes, that's exactly how it is. There is a greater difference between our parents and us.

Gunvor: Yes! It sure is. Absolutely.

Carin: Yes, it definitely is.

(Focus group, Sweden, born 1940–1945)

However, generations are not only distinguished through the marking of distance and generation gaps but there are also what could be called generational reproduction patterns of media use, such as when informants relate to older generations' media use that has been inherited.

Radio, for example, is not only connected to those generations who came of age when radio was the dominant medium, before the arrival of television. It is also present among younger cohorts, but yet again it seemingly means something else compared to what it does to the older groups. There are several accounts in the interviews where radio is mentioned as a link to the older generations, and some of the interviewees describe how they listen to radio with parents or grandparents, or that habits are generationally reproduced:

Marju: I wake up with Kuku radio every morning, I have no TV. I set the alarm so that the radio turns on just as the news begin. I listen to it… it always says the most important things and I will know if a war has broken out in the world.

Interviewer: Why do you prefer Kuku radio?

Marju: It's a habit from childhood. As far back as I can remember, my parents have always listened to Kuku radio.

(Estonian focus group, born 1990–1995)

Similar accounts can also include cultural influences from older siblings, from whom one has borrowed records, for example. Such intergenerational bridging can also jump one generation, as we shall see in the next chapter.

Conclusions

This chapter has presented an analysis of the relationship between the structural frameworks of the 'objective' media landscape of the twentieth and twenty-first centuries, and the various 'subjective' landscapes described in focus groups of Swedish and Estonian generations. The approach has been both intergenerational and cross-cultural, and the ambition has been to understand the components that produce cultural and generational differences and similarities.

First, and as an empirical conclusion of the intercultural comparison, it is obvious and very expected that the two dramatically different contexts in the media landscapes (technologically and organisationally), in geo-politics and in cultural traditions make the Swedish and Estonian generations different. For each cohort different societal events are remembered, and the different media systems produce different generational responses between the two countries. The 'objective' media landscapes (and, for that matter, political and cultural landscapes) naturally have a strong impact on the generational experience. The differences stand out irrespective of the generation on which we are focusing, but the differences are larger and more profound when it comes to the generations that have lived the better parts of their lives under Soviet occupation. This was, of course, also a time when the objective landscapes were the most different, so it can be highly expected that experiences vary accordingly. But there are also tenacious cultural legacies that follow the younger Estonian generations despite the fact that the objective landscapes have become more similar.

Second, and following from this, there are obvious differences across the different generations, in both Sweden and Estonia. These differences can, on the one hand, be attributed to the different media landscapes in which the two generations were brought up, as referred to in the first point above. The Estonian generation born in the early 1940s struggled with reading old books with Gothic letters at their relatives' homes, while the Swedish corresponding generation remember children's radio programmes. In both Sweden and Estonia this generation also refer to media used by their parents (foremost radio and press). The early 1960s generation in both Sweden and Estonia more homogeneously related their experiences to television, although for the Swedish generation this was blended with comics and music, while the Estonians related to cinema and also to music. So, also expectedly, the differences were greater between the early 1940s generations in Sweden and Estonia, while there were more similarities between those born in the early 1960s, with television as the common denominator, and subsequently the differences that can be related to the objective media landscape diminish the closer to the present we are.

The specific generational experience is marked both by the social context of the interview situation and those moments where the participants find common habits or experiences. But it is also formed more explicitly in references to older or younger persons, for example, when participants in the interview refer to older persons as being less capable of understanding new media technologies, or the failure to find any meaning in the younger people spending so much time online. This internal congregation versus external distinction works as a dialectic in the generationing process.

Theoretically, then, it can be concluded that generation as locality needs to consider not only *temporal locality* in the historical process, but also *spatial locality*: that is, the locality of geo-political, media technological and cultural space. In terms of fresh contact, and formative years, it can further be concluded that there are two kinds of formative years: one in childhood and one in youth. While Mannheim held the latter to be more important, it is clear from the focus group interviews referred to above that childhood memories also have a formative experiential dimension, and are important for the self-construction of generation as actuality. And even if these memories are more subjective than the collective experiences in youth, they bring in the dimension of age, life course and situation to the generational experience in a qualitatively different way compared to the youth experience. Thus, they also contribute to the process of generationing. This interrelation between age, life course and life situation, and generation is an avenue that will be further explored in the next chapter.

Notes

1   In addition to the societal events and the arrival of new media technologies, two quantitative datasets were used in order to identify breaking points in media use among users related to year of birth. For a detailed account of the methodology, see Opermann (2014).

2   The idea of 'Folkhemmet' (The People's Home) was established in Sweden in the 1920s when the social democratic party, in competition with conservatives, won the 'discursive battle over the term *folk'*, a battle that for example in Germany was won by the Nazis (Becker et al. 2000: 9). From the 1930s through the 1970s, the social democrats dominated Swedish politics with a mix of 'modernism with tradition', comprising among other things a high degree of 'social engineering' (Becker et al. 2000: 11). This social engineering was to a high degree centred on the concept of 'home', not least as the political programme emphasised the need for new housing conditions. Efforts were made to replace the old and often poor housing areas with new houses, giving way to light, spacious, functionalist apartments in the inner cities and their surrounding suburbs.

3   The logotype can be seen at http://muuseum.err.ee/content/fafe9453-810a-40fb-add0-e7dbbea77af4 (accessed 26 November 2013).

4 A clip can be found at www.youtube.com/watch?v=Grws71nIFpc (accessed 26 November 2013).

5 In 1971 Yleisradio built a new television transmitter in Finland, which meant that about a third of Estonians could access Western popular culture. In addition, in 1979 a new television tower was built in Tallinn, and people could then watch Estonian TV, Central TV (Russian) 1 and 2, Leningrad TV (Russian), and the Finnish channels YLE 1 and YLE 2.

6 See: www.imdb.com/title/tt1421032/plotsummary?ref_=tt_ov_pl (accessed 26 November 2013).

7 For its 60th anniversary, the newspaper *Postimees* published a review: www.postimees. ee/216738/lasteajakiri-taheke-peab-50-sunnipaeva (accessed 26 November 2013).

8 *Valgus Koordis* is an Estonian film classic from 1951. In the Internet Movie Database it is dismissed as a typical propaganda film: 'About forming first collective-farms in Estonia in 1940s and class-fight in the countryside. Starring unforgettable opera singer Georg Ots. A pretty good example of a Soviet propaganda film. No cinematographic value.' (www. imdb.com/title/tt0447516/). There are several excerpts on YouTube.

9 *The Great Waltz* (1938) is a musical loosely based on the biography of Johann Strauss II. Several clips exist on YouTube.

10 It is not entirely clear what Urve is referring to here, but a possible interpretation of this is that the young girls were eager to see a Russian movie (and to be present from the start) and that Karla Savi expressed his scorn for the Soviet propaganda. It seems as if the girls thought that any movie was better than no movie. (Thanks to Signe Opermann for suggesting this explanation.)

5

NOSTALGIA AND THE PROCESS OF GENERATIONING

If Chapter 4 focused on the importance of cultural space for the generational experience, then Chapter 5, as the next to last chapter, deals with temporal features, exemplified by the notion of nostalgia and its role in the process of generationing. It will be argued, using interview material, that nostalgia comes in different shapes, some of which have to do with early childhood memories, where media often play a significant role (children's stories, radio programmes, etc.), frequently combined with significant personal experiences such as being hospitalised, or connected to everyday family life. Other types of nostalgia are more related to the formative years of youth (the late teens and early twenties), where popular culture and music plays a significant role. This second type of nostalgia is also at the root of what could be called generational gaps, as it often appears among parents when their children move towards the end of *their* formative years. Here the impossibility of generational knowledge transfer becomes obvious, as well as the impossibility of sharing the sentiments from youth with one's own children. In this latter nostalgia, revealed in collective modes (such as the focus group interview), the childhood nostalgia is highly individualised and related to a more general loss of childhood and ageing.

Passion and nostalgia

One component in the generational experience strongly related to media is the intimate and often passionate relationship that is developed towards media technologies and content from one's formative youth period. In audience studies, a large body of work relates to fans and other media users who are passionately engaged, seeking pleasure in and receiving empowerment from their object of desire (e.g. Harrington & Bielby 1995, Harris & Alexander 1998, Hills 2002, Jenkins 2006b, Pearson 2009). The objects of passionate desire naturally vary with the times, and some stars, idols and celebrities stay longer in the limelight than others, which means that they might become the object of desire for different generations.

Passion, however, is a dialectic concept that not only refers to the joyful desire and intense emotional engagement with cherished objects but also includes its dialectic opposite in the form of pain and suffering. The reference to pain and suffering stems from its origins in Christianity, and etymologically the concept comes from the Greek verb πάσχω (*paschō*), and from classical Latin *passiōn*, *passiō* – to suffer. Here, passion refers to the last hours in the life of Jesus Christ, from his entering the temple in Jerusalem, to his betrayal, the Last Supper, the Garden of Gethsemane, imprisonment, his flogging by the guards, his dragging the cross to Golgotha, his crucifixion and death – events that are described in the four Gospels of Matthew, Mark, Luke and John in the New Testament, and which have been the object of much debate and interpretation in Theology and Biblical Studies (for an authoritative review of the debate, see Brown 1994). This part of passion is entirely absent from the fan and audience literature.

Nostalgia as a phenomenon shares the dual quality of bliss and pain with passion. In fact, one could argue that nostalgia is a specific form of passion, directed towards past passionate moments, or at least past moments of significance in a person's life course. Clearly nostalgia can take many forms, ranging from the everyday conception where it often simply connotes cultural preference for something from the past, a 'universal catchword for looking back' as David Lowenthal (1985: 4) phrases it, to its origins in clinical diagnoses. The concept first appears in medicine in the late seventeenth century, in a dissertation by the Swiss doctor Johannes Hofer, where it is described as 'the desire to return to one's native homeland' (quoted in Boym 2001: 3). Hofer derived it from the combination of the Greek words νόστος (*nóstos*), meaning 'homecoming', and άλγος (*álgos*), meaning 'pain', or 'ache', and used it to analyse the specific form of homesickness that Swiss soldiers were confronted with during service abroad in Italy and France.

As James Phillips (1985) has pointed out, the 'homesickness' described in the clinical literature from 1688 and onwards soon gave way to another meaning of the concept, that was more related to time than to space: where nostalgia as homesickness deals with the actual separation of a person from his or her home (land), present-day nostalgia refers to a displacement in time – the yearning for 'lost time', to cite the person perhaps most associated with nostalgia, Marcel Proust (1913/1996). Philips, then, contrasts the exile and homesickness of Odysseus with the internalised, symbolic homesickness of nostalgia, and points out that the main difference is that 'space is retraversable, while time is not, the return is possible for the homesick exile in a way that it is not for the nostalgic' (Philips 1985: 65). In fact, Philips holds, one can read the fate of Odysseus both ways. Odysseus does indeed return to Ithaka after twenty years, but

> Odysseus does not fully return, as he finds his home but not his youth. And even his home has been altered by time. The temporal loss is thus more profound, always encroaching on the spatial sphere.
>
> *(Philips 1985: 65)*

Being nostalgic, then, is ultimately tragic, as time is irrecoverably lost. It is a 'mourning for the impossibility of mythical return, for the loss of an enchanted world with clear borders and values' (Boym 2001: 8). But it also brings joyful memories. Nostalgia in this sense aims to capture the kind of bittersweet remembrance of something past, something that one longs for at the same time as one knows that this moment is impossible to regain. In Svetlana Boym's (2001: 1) phrasing, it is the 'hypochondria of the heart', it is the trigger of 'involuntary memory' (Proust), activated by, for example, the taste of a madeleine cake – or a prompting question in a focus group interview.

In a similar way to Philips, Svetlana Boym also distinguishes between two types or 'tendencies' of nostalgia, which each emphasise either time or space, respectively. *Restorative nostalgia* deals more with *nóstos* than with *álgos*, and seeks to reconstruct the old home, and 'patch up the memory gaps', whereas *reflective nostalgia* is more about álgos, about 'longing and loss' (Boym 2001: 41). Restorative nostalgics, argues Boym, do not consider their approach nostalgic, but about truth, and this type of nostalgia can be found in diverse national movements in the contemporary: while restorative nostalgia 'manifests itself in total reconstructions of monuments of the past, reflective nostalgia lingers on ruins' (p. 41).

In this chapter the discussion on the subjective and experiential dimension of generation building will be extended and deepened in order to more fully account for generation as actuality, and the mechanisms by which it is formed. I will do so by discussing passion and nostalgia as components in the formation of generational experience. This discussion is conducted using focus group and individual interview data with Swedish and Estonian media users of different ages and generations, read through the theoretical lens of reflective nostalgia and passion, in order to understand its role in the formation of a generational experience and the process of generationing. The advantages of the concepts of passion and nostalgia are related to their dialectic character of pleasure and pain, and the existential dimensions that such an analytical perspective opens up. Passion, it will be argued, is activated by the nostalgic relationships to past media experiences, the bittersweet remembrances of media habits and other formative objects and events connected to earlier points in life.

Given that individuals grow up at different points in 'cosmic time' as represented by the external time of the calendar (Ricouer 1985/1990), one can expect to find differences in each person's experiences as expressed by people that have grown up in different media and socio-political landscapes. In order to get to the generational experience as perceived by different birth cohorts (as potential generations), cosmic time needs thus to be complemented with Ricoeur's notion of 'lived time': that is, the specific time where moments in our lives are given meaning, and where some moments are perceived as more meaningful than others. These intensified moments of meaning-making are also potentially those in relation to which nostalgic memories are formed, and can thus be incorporated in the general self-understanding of people as belonging to a generationally defined social formation.

The variation in the formation of the generational experience among media users needs to be understood not only in relation to the cosmic time external to the individual but also in relation to the objective structures of the media landscapes where different historical trajectories produce differences in the media systems in various national and cultural contexts. Such variations, as we have seen in previous chapters, concern both the media *technologies* of each system as well as the *content*, and the organisational principles for its distribution. One might thus expect that individuals born around the same time, and in the same geo-cultural, political and media landscape should develop similar relationships to the media as technologies and content. Some of these relationships will have a nostalgic character, and in the next section three types of such nostalgic modes will be discussed. These modes will then in a subsequent section be related to the generationing process in order to explain how a generational we-sense is developed. The modes have been extracted from the same interview material with Swedish and Estonian media users that was used in Chapter 4.

Passionate and nostalgic modes

Nostalgia, argue Emily Keightley and Michael Pickering in their book *The Mnemonic Imagination*, can take many forms, and is 'a pervasive feature of modern cultural dynamics' (Keightley & Pickering 2012: 113). Keightley and Pickering conceptualise nostalgia as formed on the basis of the three 'constituents' of loss, lack and longing, where 'longing is an orientation to the past from the perspective of the present, lack is oriented to the present and an absence within it'. As they explain:

> [T]he experience of loss creates an awareness of lack, and feelings antecedent to nostalgia may then arise out of the realisation that the lack cannot be made good because what has been lost is now unregainable.
>
> *(Keightley & Pickering 2012: 117)*

Such intersections of temporality, it will be argued below, makes some forms of nostalgia important features in the generationing process, and in this section shall be discussed some of the ways in which these features operate. In the rest of the chapter three types of nostalgic modes will be discussed – technostalgia, nostalgia as loss of childhood, and nostalgia as the (im)possibility of intergenerational experience. They are not mutually exclusive, but while there are overlaps, there are also distinct qualities that separate them as specific forms of experience. Where technostalgia, for example, has tactile dimensions that to a certain extent can be reproduced (that is, re-experienced), the other two aspects are more related to irrecoverable loss. In that respect they are also more painful. Neither are they exhaustive, and there are several accounts in Keightley and Pickering's book that extend beyond the examples given here, for instance what they call 'retrotyping', or 'designer pastness' (Keightley & Pickering 2012: 150ff): that is, marketing strategies that play on nostalgia (Pickering & Keightley 2014). This kind of commercial nostalgia includes not only advertising that plays on older advertising clips but also designs of bars and restaurants (Kalinina 2014). Retrotyping is, however, a type of 'regressive nostalgia' that does not contain all of the three constituent parts that Keightley and Pickering theorise, since they only appeal to the component of backwards longing, and 'conceal or deny the loss and painful sense of lack which elsewhere are its other two components' (Pickering & Keightley 2014: 84). Such nostalgic forms that are only engaging in the joyful or blissful side of nostalgia (at the expense of the painful side) are of less interest in a discussion of the process of generationing, since they are more involved in the management of moods and contexts that are presumably more superficial and related to specific moments. These forms of nostalgia do not touch on the existential dimensions of nostalgia and passion, and this type of what could be called 'nostalgia light' is, therefore, left out in this context.

The commercial exploitation of this more superficial form of nostalgia seems to be endless, and it can also appear in many forms. There is, for example, a large collection of books produced about past consumer objects and media phenomena that have been popular for a specific birth cohort. Typically these are given away as birthday presents when friends celebrate their thirtieth or fortieth birthday, to the amusement of all friends of the same age, and one can jokingly remember the ugliness of V-jeans, disco music and TV commercials. Such forms of commercial nostalgia also include what Amy Holdsworth (2011: 98f) calls 'list television' or 'archive television', that is, television shows that build on archival clips directed to niche audiences of a specific age who presumably want to engage in trips down memory lane. Such nostalgic flirtations with the television audience seem to cross national boundaries and appear in similar forms in many countries across the world, although each individual show will draw on explicitly national archival material. Thus we can see *Starie Pesni o Glavnom* in Russia (Kalinina 2014: 98ff), a whole range of 'best of…' shows in Britain (Holdsworth 2011: 99), or *Minnenas television* in Sweden.

Archival productions are naturally not restricted to television but are equally present on the Internet, and include websites with links to merchandise or music, such as those that focus on the early 1970s on *In the 1970s* (www.inthe70s.com/); one can have a more nation-specific memory trip with *Reminisce This – A very British nostalgia site* (www.reminiscethis.co.uk/) or the YouTube channel *Nostalgic Television* (www.youtube.com/user/TheButler191), or take the full tour on *Nostalgia Central*, that aims to cover nostalgia from a wide range of time periods with the promise to be:

> your one stop reference guide through five decades of music, movies, television, pop culture and social history – from the rockin' fifties, via the swinging sixties, the mirror-balled seventies, and the day-glo eighties, to the Britpop nineties.
>
> *(nostalgiacentral.com)*

Some would argue that we are witnessing a 'nostalgia wave' that cuts across television and the Internet (Niemeyer 2014a: 2), and this supposed heightened interest in nostalgic collections and archives among media users is naturally exploited commercially by the media and culture industries (Pickering & Keightley 2014). Katharina Niemeyer's (2014b) book on *Media and Nostalgia* collects a wide range of examples of media technologies and nostalgic forms, with a special focus on the nostalgic qualities of cinema, television and photography. In fact, one can note that television, and visually based media more generally, holds a prominent position in 'nostalgia studies' on media, while there is comparatively less focus on music, although naturally such studies can also be found (e.g. Finn 1992, Wickström & Steinholt 2009).

Some of this commercial output undoubtedly produces nostalgic sentiments among some people, but the prefabricated nostalgia needs to be related to by a nostalgic subject in order for nostalgia as a state of being to become realised. Until that point, it is just retrotyping. The following part of this chapter will discuss three such points where nostalgia appears in the form of technostalgia, nostalgia as loss of childhood, and nostalgia as the realisation of the impossibility of intergenerational transfer of experience.

Technostalgia

Technostalgia as a concept has been used in analyses of sound media such as valve amplifiers, vintage musical instruments, and so on, and refers to the preference for old, often analogue, technologies (Pinch & Reinecke 2009). It is, however, in previous studies (cf. several chapters in Bijsterveld & van Dijck 2009), somewhat under-theorised. In relation to the interviews analysed for this chapter, it relates, on the one hand, to first-hand experiences of the use of media technologies (rather than content), and, on the other hand, to media that evoke social relations and situations.

First, technostalgia is directed towards now 'outdated' communication forms such as letter writing (the phenomenon of 'pen pals') – a yearning for a kind of pre-digital connectedness that precedes contemporary social networking media such as Facebook (that the younger generations engage in). But it is also directed towards other media technologies such as comics, cassette tapes and vinyl records, some of which have been replaced by digital alternatives. It is partly a mourning of dead media technologies in themselves, but it is also the gradual disappearing tangible materiality of the media that produces nostalgic remembrance: an emotional attachment to the 'rustly' sounds when reading the print newspaper, the memories triggered by LP album covers, and mix tapes. This nostalgia is clearly social, for example when the focus group participants turn to each other to ask 'Do you remember…?' or when they seek to establish social confirmation by enthusiastically agreeing 'yes, yes' to their bygone, mutually shared experiences.

Nostalgia in this form is seldom connected to content in itself, since content today obviously lives on and can reappear on many platforms of consumption, whereas the technologies disappear, or become more difficult to use (for example, where do you buy cassette tapes nowadays?). Several respondents report on having exchanged their record collections several times over the years, from vinyl discs to

CDs, MP3s and then hard-drives and streaming services. The old media are not thrown away, however, but stored away in attics and cellars as an archive of bygone events and feelings. It is not *any* version of a certain song or album, but the *specific* copy of a *specific* record (the vinyl copy with the original cover) that is the trigger of memories and emotional states.

> Marie: As I see it, today you lose the value in it… my children would think I am silly now, I know, but… because, when you went and bought a vinyl record with a cover. You *do* remember the covers of certain records still, don't you? And you remember the feeling when you bought it, and what it stood for.
>
> *(Focus group, Sweden, born 1962–1964)*

Technostalgia, as seen from the quote, is about the unique quality of the medium, but is also clearly connected to a specific emotional state of the individual.

Secondly, technostalgia is also related to labour investment; a mix tape, for example, is 'something you put an effort into making' (Mats, born 1962–1964), and 'has a stronger meaning because it's a physical thing' (Marie, born 1962–1964). These formulations reappear in several of the focus groups of different age cohorts:

> *Linda*: I always listened to *Trackslistan* on Saturdays, and you recorded it because you wanted the songs. And so you paused in between the songs, and… 'Shit, now the talk was recorded again!' And then you had to rewind. That was the main thing. And then you could listen to the hits afterwards.
>
> *Jonas*: I had this double cassette player and edited so I got the tunes I wanted, and then I cut away what I didn't want to have, like talk and such things.
>
> *(Focus group, Sweden, born 1977–1980)*

An interesting fact is that the practice of making mix tapes was remembered in so many of the focus groups, across birth cohorts. The cassette tape as a medium was clearly approaching its 'best before' date during the formative years of the respondents in the youngest generation, aged 15–20 years old, who were born in the early 1990s when cassette tapes successively became replaced by digital recording technology. At this time, the vinyl record had already been exchanged for CDs, and soon MP3 players, iPods, and so on. However, the labour invested in creating mix tapes on cassette was imprinted in their memories, in the same way as it was for older generations.

> *Frida*: I recorded mix tapes on cassette. Tried to avoid the commercials and mix songs together.
>
> *Interviewer*: I see, and then you recorded from the radio?
>
> *Frida*: Yes, exactly. You have to stay alert so you don't record the commercials, and try to make a good mix.

Interviewer: Do you still have those tapes?

Frida: Yes, in fact I do.

David: Cool!

Frida: There is so much hard work behind each one. They are still there in the drawer.

(*Focus group, Sweden, born 1991–1995*)

The mix tape is indeed one of the paradigmatic triggers of memory (cf. Jansen 2009), as seen in the quotes above. One could argue that this is because it was one of the first media technologies that allowed for the user to become a small producer – an early form of what today is cherished as the 'produser' quality of new digital media. Admittedly, there were other technologies of production that preceded the cassette tape, such as Double- and Super-8 amateur film, or indeed the 'traditional' open-reel tape recorders. Amateur film-making was possible already in the beginning of the twentieth century (Zimmermann 1995), open-reel tape recorders despite a long prehistory were not widespread until the 1950s when the invention of electromagnetic tape made them more suitable for amateurs (Nyre 2009: 113ff). Both the amateur film medium and the open-reel tape recorder were more media for enthusiasts, and tape recording did not become widespread among general media users until the 1970s, when the cassette tape recorder made acquiring a tape recorder more affordable for young persons.

However, the accessibility of cassette tape recorders is not what is emphasised by media users. The ease with which one can work the technology is never mentioned in the interviews, and cassette tapes are never contrasted to the more expensive and complicated technology of open-reel tape recorders. What is mentioned is the labour investment. The labour laid down in producing a mix tape, either for oneself or for a cherished or loved other, obviously produces a cultural value that is bound to the individual (Bolin 2011). Furthermore, this is a labour that is *not* based in alienation, and from the quotes it is obvious that the work that is laid down is not *any* work, it is not abstract work in Marx's sense, but concrete, individualised and specifically personal work that can be tied to a specific individual. The mix tape has a 'stronger meaning' in contrast to other prefabricated tapes because of the 'effort' and the 'hard work'. To receive a mix tape from someone means that the person really has made an effort in planning, selecting, carefully editing songs in a collection directed at one special individual, for example a prospective boy- or a girlfriend. English best-selling author Nick Hornby describes the labour involved in producing such a mix tape in his 1995 book *High Fidelity*:

> To me, making a tape is like writing a letter – there's a lot of erasing and rethinking and starting again. A good compilation tape, like breaking up, is hard to do. You've got to kick off with a corker, to hold the attention (I started with 'Got to Get You Off My Mind', but then realised that she might not get any further than track one, side one if I delivered what she wanted straightaway, so I buried it in the middle of side two), and then you've got to

up it a notch, or cool it a notch, and you can't have white music and black music together, unless the white music sounds like black music, and you can't have two tracks by the same artist side by side, unless you've done the whole thing in pairs and... oh, there are loads of rules.

(Hornby 1995: 96)

One of the reasons of the immediate popularity of *High Fidelity* is most likely because many people across several generations and in various cultural spaces, have recognised themselves in the almost obsessive youthful devotion to music that the book is centred on. This is probably also why it was adapted for the cinema with such ease in 2000; the film was directed by British director Stephen Frears and with US actor John Cusack in the leading role. The shift of the setting from London to Chicago seems to have mattered little to its popularity as it is the more international sentiment in relation to music consumption (and the production of mix tapes) that is the main focus of the film, and produces what Ien Ang (1982/1991) in the context of television soap opera viewing has called an 'emotional realism' that audiences can relate to.

Although mix tapes are seldom produced in order to trigger memories later in life, they receive this function, and become a 'frozen mirror' that makes it possible to '[encounter] a previous self' (Jansen 2009: 44). Mix-taping as a practice was at its peak between the late 1970s and early 1990s, up until the point when the possibility of burning CDs became widespread. Although it is also possible to burn music mixes on CDs, this practice does not seem to produce either the emotions or the labour intensity that the mix tapes did. It is less labour intensive, less personal and, hence, seems to have less value.

For the youngest generation in Sweden, this resembles the analogue nostalgia theorised by Laura Marks, but is more connected to the investment in labour in producing them. Analogue nostalgia, in Marks' perspective, deals less with the emotional labour invested in compiling mix tapes, and has more to do with the 'indexical' quality of the sound, 'a retrospective fondness for the "problems" of decay and generational loss that analogue video posed' (Marks 2002: 152). Her analysis is, however, made against a specific educational setting of media production, where she finds that 'analogue nostalgia seems especially prevalent among works by students who started learning video production when it was fully digital' (p. 153). The question is, however, if this really is nostalgia at all: can one long for a home where one has never lived? Is this not rather a *phantom pain* caused by a more general fascination with preforms of the present technologies? In terms of home, this means longing for someone else's home – a specific kind of *nostalgic envy* of the home one never had.

Nostalgia as loss of childhood

Nostalgic remembrances directed at childhood media use appear in all generations, even among those who were in their formative years at the time of the interview. Vinyl records are connected to childhood memories, but the memories are not technostalgic: that is, not directed towards the technology but rather towards the content. For the youngest Estonian generation, this can be seen in traditional child-hood favourites such as the characters Toots and Kiir from the cult classics *Kevade* ('Spring') and *Suvi* ('Summer'), based on the novels by Estonian author Oskar Luts from 1912 and onwards. These were released on LP records in 1969 and 1971, respec-tively, and have been immensely popular among generations of Estonian children.[1] Toots and Kiir could never have been experienced first-hand by this generation, since the records arrived several years before they were born, but are rather remem-bered as 'classics'. But it is also clear that it is the quality of the stories as laid down on vinyl that is the trigger of nostalgia, and a social loss of family life in childhood.

Among the Swedish generations, childhood memories are most often connected to children's radio programmes (for the generation born in the early-1940s) and children's television shows (for the generations born in the early-1960s, late-1970s and early-1990s). For the early-1940s generation, however, this seems not to be connected with nostalgic remembrances. But, especially for the Estonian genera-tion born in the early 1960s, several children's programmes are mentioned, such as *Telepoiss, Entel-Tentel* or *Tipp ja Täpp*.

Sometimes the memories are related to important life-history events, such as spending time in hospital. Mare, born in 1940, vividly remembers when she was in hospital with diphtheria at the age of four, and how she received Hans Christian Andersen's tale of Thumbelina, written 1835 and published in 1956 in Estonia as *Pöial-Liisi*, with characteristic drawings by Estonian illustrator Siima Škop. The mem-ory of having received *Pöial-Liisi* from her aunt was clearly the marker of an import-ant life event for Mare, given that she was so young when she was hospitalised. However, this is also a distorted memory, or what Alison Landsberg (1995) would call a 'prosthetic memory', because when Mare aged four, the Thumbelina tale had not yet been published in Estonia. Mare retrospectively adjusts her media memory to include *Pöial-Liisi*. No doubt she was hospitalised at that age (she would hardly mistake her four-year-old self for her 16-year-old self), and most likely she received a book from her aunt, but she replaces that gift with *Pöial-Liisi,* which is a very famous and cherished book among Estonian children. Mare simply reinforces, or potentiates, her memory with this well-known book according to the principle that nostalgia is rarely about 'the past as actually experienced' but rather 'the past as imagined, as idealized through memory [...] by desire's distortions and reorganisations' (Hutcheon 2000: 195). And the sentiments produced by this memory are equally as real as they would have been had she actually received that book in that moment.

All nostalgic memories are, however, not related to very distant events. The younger cohorts can also report on nostalgic media moments, such as the young interviewee Valev in the quote below:

> I have very few memories. As regards TV, I remember the family watching the news. I still feel nostalgic when I turn on Vikerraadio before nine in the evening. In my first years of school mother always said that I had to go to bed at nine. Vikerraadio was always playing in the background, playing a

lullaby and a bedtime story. The best thing was that when I came from a choir rehearsal in Tallinn three or four years ago and the bus got back at nine. I just got home when they played the theme song. I loved it.

(Focus group Estonia, born 1990–1995)

In the quote Valev is referring to the children's bedtime story programme *Õhtujutt lastele* and its lead theme. This programme has been broadcast since the mid-1960s and has thus been popular among several generations of Estonian children (Roomets 2013). Consequently, it also features in other Estonian interviews, with older generational cohorts:

Aire: I would like to add that there was a bedtime story.

Ruth: I remember it too.

Aire: I think they still use the signature.

Helle: Yes, they do.

Toomas: Yes.

Helle: It is still my favourite show.

Toomas [reciting in a soft, tender voice]: 'Mom is still busy in the kitchen, I don't want to fall asleep yet...'

Aire: Yes, that's the one! And on TV there was this *Tipp ja Täpp*. And the Teleboy marched across the screen, and I think there was a girl too.

Helle: The Teleboy. *Tipp and Täpp* were from another show.

Aire: Yes, yes. *Tipp ja Täpp* was a programme. It was such...

Toomas: That was later.

Aire: Yes, and the bedtime story.

[...]

NN [unidentified female]: The song was also along these lines... 'Everyone going to sleep'.

Toomas: Yes. A time for peaceful play.

Aire: Yes, yes, yes.

Toomas: Yes, yes, indeed... I can remember everything very clearly. I can even hear this particular song [in my head].

(Focus group, Estonia, born 1959–1966)

This type of nostalgia as loss of childhood is – especially when, as in this case, it transgresses different generational cohorts – not really part of the generationing process because it does not distinguish between the experiences of previous generations from subsequent ones. It is more part of a general nostalgia directed to one's childhood and early youth. In itself it is, therefore, less of a feature in the generationing process, unless it becomes coupled with younger generations. There are, however, more collective forms of remembering, especially related to the music of one's formative youth years.

Music has, in fact, always had a prominent place in the analysis of nostalgia, from the clinical diagnosis of Hofer, to the more individualised memories of today: 'The music of home, whether a rustic cantilena or a pop song, is the permanent accompaniment to nostalgia' (Boym 2001: 4, cf. van Dijck 2009). Music has the ability to trigger memory (Davidson and Garrido 2014), which leads to nostalgic contemplation of the past: 'Yes, yes, indeed… I can remember everything very clearly. I can even hear this particular song [in my head]', as the male informant exclaimed in relation to the main theme for a children's television programme in the quote above.

Music, then, is 'a catalyst for remembering particular events, people, emotions, and places', and thus it holds a prominent position in memory studies (Stevens 2015: 264). It has the ability to produce what psychologists have termed a 'reminiscence bump' (Rubin et al. 1986), where events from one's youth and early adulthood remain in the memory of older persons to a much higher degree than events encountered later in life (cf. Rubin et al. 1998). It has also been discovered that positive memories (as opposed to negative experiences such as death or accidents in the family) acquired during this phase of life remain with one into old age to a much higher degree. Furthermore, events that can be described as 'milestones in the conventional life story' tend to be over-represented in older people's account of their 'life stories' (Steiner et al. 2014: 1008). There is also psychological research to back up the idea that Proustean 'involuntary memories' form 'a clear bump' around the age of 20, especially if they are 'happy or important memories' (Berntsen & Rubin 2002: 647), while the 'sad or traumatic' involuntary memories peak at more recent dates (p. 649). This research also points to the social dimension of memory:

> It is consistent with the assumption that autobiographical memory is organised by culturally shared life scripts that do not include emotionally negative events while allocating important positive events to young adulthood.
>
> *(Berntsen & Rubin 2002: 649)*

Such findings are well in line with Mannheim's idea of formative years, despite the ontological differences between the disciplines of cognitive psychology and sociology. The preferred methodological approach in psychological memory research is autobiographically oriented, experimental studies focusing on events of individual importance, whereas sociologists focus on collective memories related to 'national and world events' (Schuman & Corning 2014: 147). While there seem to be different ideas on the age at which 'bump' memories exactly peak, both psychologists and sociologists of memory agree that the years around 20 are the most important.

Of special interest in the context of nostalgia is the research focusing on the reminiscence bump related to music. Memory researchers have even asked if musical memories are more special than other memories (Stevens 2015). And it indeed seems as if musical memories leave a strong mark on memories from ones youth. Morris Holbrook and Robert Schindler have, for example, found that musical taste among individuals peaked at around the age of 24, after which it stagnated. The style of music that a person preferred at that age was thus most likely to stay with the individual for the rest of his or her life (Holbrook & Schindler 1989). Some of the research on music and memory has analysed that question in relation to the reminiscence bump. In a study on music and memory, Carol Krumhansl and Justin Zupnick (2013) analyse reminiscence bumps, where taste in music is not only found to be established around the age of 20, but is also reproduced across generations from the parents' generation to their children's generation. They found that the music that was popular when the researched subject's parents were aged around 20 years was also remembered and appreciated, something they attribute to what they call 'cascading reminiscence bumps'.

Empirical examples of the power of music to evoke past feelings are not hard to find. The Norwegian author Tore Renberg has, for example, eloquently described the affective impact that the music from his youth has on him today in terms of bodily reactions. Pondering his own relationship with a specific LP record – *Synd*, by the Swedish rock band Imperiet – he vividly explains:

> If I play the record today, I can feel it in my body; both what's happening in the music and *what it has done to me*. My blood runs faster, there's crackles in my temples. Each and all of my days during these first months of 1987 are summoned, and they respond back to me from the time when this album basically was the only thing I listened to.
>
> *(Renberg 2015, emphasis in original, my translation)*

This testimony is illustrative of the prominent position that music has during the formative years of youth, and the power it holds over the course of life and how music can reconnect a person with earlier emotional states and earlier selves as perceived from the horizon of the present. Such a longing for encounters with the past takes many forms, among them the engagement in dance and music evenings with 'old-time' music for older people, where one can meet with coevals and create a temporary we-sense – if only for that specific occasion (cf. Sūna 2013).

Nostalgia as the (im)possibility of intergenerational experience

A third type of nostalgia is that which concerns intergenerational experiences, or the lack thereof. The example with Toots and Kiir above illustrates the intergenerational transfer that appears when children pick up the records of their parents' generation. This example, then, has a double meaning that, apart from the loss of childhood, also points to the successful sharing of generational experience. There are several such examples in the interviews, where children discover their parents' old mix tapes, and want to 'inherit' these.

Mats: Well, now, I had thrown most of them away, but I did save some. And then my son bought an old car with a cassette player in it. And he said "What's this?", and then we took one of my old tapes. And he almost fell over laughing, and then I had recorded… rapping… and a lot of such stuff. And he thought it was dead fun… plus a lot of old corny music, and he thought that was really great. He kept the tape. He sold the car eventually, and kept the tape. Thought that, "I'll keep this" (laughter).

Interviewer: And that was your son, right?

Mats: Yes, he bought an old car and there was a cassette player in it, and he, like, wanted to exchange it, and I said, no – keep it and I'll give you some tapes, and you can play them instead.

Interviewer: But was that because it was *your* cassette tape or was it because it was *a* cassette tape?

Mats: A cassette tape. And then because I had added talk, and stuff. Mixed it together with songs and acted DJ in-between (laughter).

(Focus group, Sweden, born 1962–1964)

Similar examples of the sharing of experience between generations are also found elsewhere in the literature on memory and media: for example, concerning the intergenerational transfer of musical taste. Typically this transfer builds on children exploring their parents' old record collections, and then picking up the same taste as their parents (cf. van Dijck 2009: 111). This intergenerational transfer relates to reproduction, but not in the technical sense of the ability to reproduce songs end-lessly, contributing to the multiplication of choice, but with reproduction of taste.

Jonas: My dad really had many records. So you just listened to them and got to hear loads of music, and that led to my picking up this [taste in music].

Interviewer: Is that something you think has influenced your taste in music?

Jonas: Yes, I definitely think so.

Interviewer: What did your father listen to?

Jonas: It was a lot of sixties music. It was naturally Beatles and such, but also Swedish bands like Tages and Hep Stars. Maybe I do not listen to this today, and not specifically to those bands, but I do notice that what I like tends to align with that kind of music a lot. So it is somewhere there, in the back of my head.

(Focus group, Sweden, born 1977–1980)

The intergenerational link to the parents' generation via taste in music has been observed in previous psychologically oriented research on music memory and nos-talgia (ter Bogt et al. 2011), and has been explained on the grounds of parents playing a specific kind of music during child-rearing, thus installing in the very young child a propensity for liking this type of music. The argument is that music 'plays a central role in childrearing cross-culturally, such as in lullabies, play songs, and teaching songs, as well as other less formal musical interactions' (Krumhansl & Zupnick 2013: 2067). This might have some truth to it, but one can also see this in light of the fact that before children and young people start buying records of their own, the only records to play in the house are those of their parents.

This type of nostalgia and passion in relation to the parents' generation leans towards the more joyful. There are, however, more painful moments in the intergenerational relationships revealed in the interviews. To Marie, the extended communication opportunities that exist today have also brought with them a generation gap, and a loss of value in communication:

> But, it's like this has to do with quantity. I mean, sometimes you lose the value in… As I see it, today you lose the value in it, because when I went and bought a vinyl record with a cover. You *do* remember the covers of certain records still, don't you? And you remember the feeling when you bought it, and what it stood for. Today they just sit online, and on Spotify, and I get totally confused, because I'm there myself, and I think… God, I can download anything and listen to it. And that stresses me out, because you somehow lose your grip on… And there they are online all the time, and all of this with three hundred friends on Facebook, or you have a whole world on your computer, and whatnot. It has to do with quantity, and you somehow lose the value in it. In everything from friendship to the music.
>
> *(Focus group, Sweden, born 1962–1964)*

This is a loss of value that has to do with the technological capacity of reproduction, and the impossibility of reproduction of taste and preference. To Marie, the youth of today – including her own children who are at the formative ages of 21 and 23 years – can never understand how it felt for Marie when she bought that specific record with that specific cover, or when she produced her own, specific and unique, mix tapes. Nor can they understand what it meant to read the comics that Marie and her generation did:

> *Marie*: My children never read comics much. In fact, I didn't get the sense that it was such a strong influence in their childhood as it was for me.

This generation gap can also be illustrated by the account of Mats in the same interview, when he slightly disappointedly describes how his children did not fully appreciate his old comics:

> *Mats*: Well, I know because I have saved all my comic magazines, so they [the children] got quite a strong dose anyway. What was a bit disappointing was that *Agent X9* and *Fantomen*, and the others, they were in black and white, and then it wasn't much fun.
>
> *(Focus group, Sweden, born 1962–1964)*

What Marie and Mats are trying to express is the generational difference between themselves and their children, and the realisation that their children, who are now at the threshold of leaving their formative years, can never appreciate comics in the way they did when they were the same age. Their media habits will soon become established without them having learnt to appreciate the same media contents and share the same feelings of 'what it stood for' as their parents. This is a loss of intergenerational knowledge transfer caused by changes in the ('objective') media landscape. It is a mourning of the ability to pass on media practices and communication experiences to one's own children, as they now are close to leaving their formative years, forming their own generational consciousness and establishing the gap where each generation 'retires into its own shell and grows distant from the other' (Halbwachs 1950/1980: 68).

This is also where the combination of generational experience with life course and life situation enters the equation. Generational experience can naturally be shared *within* one's own generation, with those who have similar experiences. But it cannot always be passed on to the next generation, and this is why this type of nostalgia is triggered at the time when the generation faces their children being at the end of their formative years, having developed their own, autonomous identity. This is the moment when one realises that one's children have developed their own relation to the world, independently of their parents, and the impossibility of the intergenerationally shared experience is manifested. This fact produces nostalgia for times that will never return, and for feelings not possible to transfer between generations.

The three types of relationships to media memories referred to above are examples of intense, most often passionate encounters with technologies and content. Technostalgia, however, partly stands out from the other two as less about loss, and more about cherished memories. Some of the memories of past experiences can in fact easily be re-enacted, such as the 'rustly' quality of print newspapers, old analogue instruments, or vinyl records (even shellac records, although these are not mentioned in the interviews). This loss – if that is indeed the right word – is of a suspended kind, and is easily remedied. The records stowed away in the attic *can* indeed be revisited, and their function is rather as an archive of past emotional states.

The two other types – loss of childhood and loss of intergenerational experience – are more profound, and deal with time irrecoverably lost. They are thus more painful, and the passion they are loaded with is also nostalgic in that they cannot be revived, as that specific home which they represent is forever changed by cosmic time: or, in the words of Svetlana Boym, by 'the modern conception of unrepeatable and irreversible time' (Boym 2001: 13). This nostalgia is also the nostalgia of generational experience in a double sense: it both binds together those who have had the same experiences in the past and binds the generation together in the present through the shared feeling of loss. It becomes a specific generational value that ties together people who appreciate this value.

We can conclude from the analysis of the three types of nostalgia that they are related to the generational experience in various ways – some more, some less. The first of these – *technostalgia* – on the one hand, concerns the longing for (often) analogue technologies from one's past, such as letter writing, traditional newspapers, vinyl records and, on the other hand, the labour investment related to old media technologies. Technostalgia is highly collective, and represents a shared media experience of people who have similar experiences of bygone or outdated media technologies. It is not found only among older generational cohorts but is also found among younger persons. Unlike the subsequent two nostalgic modes, however, technostalgia can be 'cured', as it is possible to successfully revisit old technologies (although, just like Odysseus, one revisits this 'home' as a different self).

The second type of nostalgia identified concerns the *loss of childhood*, and is revealed in the early memories of media use; it is often connected to important life-history moments such as being hospitalised, but also to cherished media moments in the form of children's radio and television programmes, representing a bygone era of childhood innocence. This type of nostalgia is highly individual, and does not trigger large discussions in the focus groups. These nostalgic remembrances can nonetheless be said to be part of the generational experience since they are homologous to other childhood memories. But they are not specifically related to the media experience, nor to the historical and contextual time, but rather to childhood per se.

Third, there is the nostalgia related to *the (im)possibility of intergenerational experience*. This type deals with experiences from the formative years, and is triggered by one's children coming towards the end of their formative years, where the separation from parents is completed. This type of nostalgia is collective, and shared among the parents in the focus groups. It is produced by the realisation that the specific experience, in the words of Wilhelm Pinder 'represents a different *period of [the] self*, which [a person] can only share with people of his own age' (Pinder 1926: 21), and where the same time or the same event is 'experienced by several generations at various stages of development' (Mannheim 1928/1952: 283).

These three forms of nostalgia are all reflexive, in Boym's terminology, as they deal more with loss and longing than with 'truth'. They are all triggered by media memories (as prompted in the interview situation), although they could in principle also have been activated by non-media prompts. These are not the only three modes of passionate media memories and nostalgic remembrances. There are – as Keightley and Pickering's example with retrotyping shows – also other modes, related to other cultural contexts, and possibly also to other generations, as each generation is confronted with their own 'objective' structures in the form of specific media and societal landscapes. Retrotyping and other forms of 'nostalgia light' are, however, not equally relevant to the generationing process, and have hence been dealt with to a much lesser degree in this context. Together with the three examples given here, one can conclude that the increased abilities to revisit media content via digital archives should make media-related analysis of passion and nostalgia as dialectical concepts that encompass the duality of blissful suffering even more interesting in future research, as that which seems irrecoverably lost today, might be, or at least might appear to be, less so in the future.

Conclusion: Life phase related nostalgia

Nostalgia, as this chapter has revealed, stands out as one important ingredient in the process of generationing since it actualises the relation between the present and the past. It is, in the words of Linda Hutcheon, 'the very pastness of the past, its inaccessibility, that likely accounts for a large part of nostalgia's power' (Hutcheon 2000: 195). Nostalgia, as we have seen, is indeed a product of the present, determined by wishes and desires that are directed backwards, towards the past as an imagined state of existence that may have only loose relations to what actually happened in childhood. This 'tiger's leap' into the past (Benjamin 1955/1999: 261) produces the memory and the experience that also confirm the generational sense of belonging.

The intergenerational differences are also clearly revealed in the nostalgic memories, where the members of the oldest generation seems more prone to relate their nostalgia to media use in childhood, while the early 1960s generation first and foremost relate to their formative years. This can be explained as a loss of the ability to achieve intergenerational transference on the part of the generation born in the early 1960s, who at the time of being interviewed could see their children leaving their formative years different from themselves, while the oldest generation interviewed displayed a loss of childhood. This might be to do with their now having grandchildren of the same age that they were when they first experienced children's literature (although evidence of this is absent in the interviews). This would then be a kind of nostalgia that is more life-phase related. If this holds true, however, we can expect the early 1960s generation to gradually move away from their nostalgia for their formative years as they become older and enter into other phases of life (such as retirement, and having grandchildren), to the benefit of childhood nostalgia. In this way the generational component would interact with age, life phase or life situation, and produce the mix of social and psychological features that impact on lives as they move through the ever-shifting 'objective' media landscapes.

More broadly, Emily Keightley and Michael Pickering argue that nostalgia is 'a direct consequence of modernity', and that it 'is a response to broad structures of social change and transformation' (Keightley and Pickering 2012: 115). This yearning for what once was is also a main ingredient in the generational self-understanding, and is thus at the same time one of the motors of social change, as it occurs between generations. This happens because nostalgia is generation specific – it is directed at previous states of existence, and these states can only appear for those who have lived through them. And just as it is true, as the saying goes, that you cannot step down into a river twice, since when you step into the water the second time it will then not be the same river, one cannot swim in the same historical current at two different points in time. Paradoxically, the longing for the past is actually producing the type of change that makes longing possible in the first place (since technologies, ways of engaging with the media, etc., need to have disappeared or been transformed if they are to merit mnemonic attention and produce nostalgia).

Longing is thus one of the motors of historical unfolding. In the next chapter the relation between historical change – including media change – and generational formation will be summarised and discussed more fully, in order to establish the role of the process of mediatised generationing in relation to the wider historical process.

Note

1 Information on the records can be found on www.ledzeppelin.ee/lisainfo.php?id=224 and www.ledzeppelin.ee/lisainfo.php?id=223.

6

GENERATION, MEDIATISATION AND THE RHYTHM OF AGES

As indicated at the beginning of this book, there is not really any shortage of generational concepts circulating within general public debate and in the academy: baby boomers, the silent generation, digital natives, Millennials, dotnets, global generations, media generations, the Facebook generation, and so on. These labels are indicative in that they point to one single defining characteristic that the generation in question is supposed to have. Accordingly there are labels referring to specific historical eras (such as is the case with Millennials or 1960s generation), to demographic conditions (baby boomers), or to specific formative historical events (the Vietnam generation, the Cold War generation), to characters of reach (global generation), or to personality traits seen as common for the generation in question (the lost generation, the silent generation, generation me).

Some of these defining characteristics are related to media. In fact, and as Nicoletta Vittadini and her colleagues have pointed out, the media 'seems to have a special allure' that makes them more fitting for labelling generations compared with other technologies (such as the 'refrigerator' or the 'dishwasher') (Vittadini et al. 2013b: 65). The media are referenced in several different ways, however. One type of reference concerns specific media technologies. Thus we have the radio generation, the TV generation, the mobile generation, and so on. Other defining characteristics relate more broadly to technological systems, especially the new digital and web-based technologies: digital natives, digital generation, dotnets, and so on. Yet other labels are very specific, such as Facebook generation, or Google generation, which should perhaps be read metaphorically as a general reference to a generation defined by its social networking media use. As an umbrella term for pointing to the impact of the media on the generational experience, the more generic term media generation has also been used (Hepp et al. 2014).

We will return to the concept of media generation to discuss it more thoroughly towards the end of this chapter. Before that some of the main points that have been discussed in the preceding empirically oriented chapters will be summarised, in order to then theoretically discuss the role of the media in generational formations and the generationing process, and the role of generations in wider processes of historical change and mediatisation. This means that the first section of the chapter sums up and comments briefly on the empirical conclusions, while the second part concerns the broader theoretical conclusions to the inquiry on media and generations, the role of the media and communication and the implications for historical change, including the mediatisation process.

Generations in historical and techno-cultural landscapes

In the preceding three chapters I have tried to build an argument based on an analytical model that relates the very structures within which generations are born and come of age to the social and collective actions of that specific generation – actions that in turn help produce structures for coming generations to act within.

Chapter 3 discussed generations in terms of them being located in the historical process of specific, nationally defined media landscapes as objective structures of media technologies and content that, in conjunction with other social conditions, the members of different birth cohorts make sense of, interpret and act in relation to. As each specific birth cohort will meet a media landscape that is different from preceding cohorts, the ways in which the assemblage of media technologies are used will also be specific for each cohort. Naturally, this also goes for the content of the media, since new genres, new formats, and new texts arrive continuously, and even if they might be argued to be variants of earlier genres, formats and texts, they will nonetheless function as distinctive markers between cohorts. To say, for example, that 'shock rocker' Marilyn Manson's performances are just replicas of everything Alice Cooper did in the early 1970s is to miss the point here, since these two artists are talking to different age cohorts. In fact, the debate itself should be seen as a marker of generational distinction. Thus, when those who were in their formative youth years in the 1970s and admired Alice Cooper dismiss Marilyn Manson as a replica, they just confirm their out-group status in relation to those who appreciate Manson.

The same chapter also gave an empiric example where mobile phone use among young people in Sweden and Estonia was discussed in terms of cohort-based user patterns that could presumably be indicative of common approaches and possible generationally founded understandings of the media. This analysis revealed the different approaches that different birth cohorts have to new media technologies in terms of how various functions on the mobile are used. This analysis was also cross-cultural and illustrated the importance of historical user patterns for contemporary media habits, where the different access structures and user patterns differed between Sweden and Estonia, which has led to the development of different ways of using the mobile.

The analysis in Chapter 3 mainly builds on quantitative, statistical data. Such data can illustrate differences in access, use and preferences between birth cohorts as statistical aggregates, but cannot say much about experience. Differences in media user patterns are, of course, indicators of attitudes specific to a generational consciousness and can be used for those purposes in the analysis. However, if one wants more elaborate discursive material that will capture perceptions, memories and experiences, then one has to rely on interviews or written accounts, which are the main methods used in Chapters 4 and 5.

Chapter 4 demonstrated some of the ways in which individuals and groups make sense of, act and also represent their action in these landscapes, and how one can observe a generational we-sense appear when media users relate to their early media memories. When accounting for these memories, media users also directly and indirectly relate their own location in the historical process to that of preceding and succeeding generations, something that becomes an important feature in the process of generationing. First, a pair-wise cross-cultural comparison between four different generational groups interviewed in Sweden and Estonia was made, emphasising similarities and differences in approach to media and societal events. For the two oldest groups that were interviewed (born in the early 1940s and the early 1960s), the backdrops of the post-war situation and the Cold War were contextual societal features that were common in the focus groups in both countries. Naturally, there were different approaches towards the societal conditions, pointing to different generation units by way of different responses, but the general post-war and Cold War situation made a strong impact as reported in the interviews in both countries. This is also consistent with Signe Opermann's (2014) findings based on quantitative data, where the older of the Estonian generations had much more homogeneous preferences when it came to (news) media, and a more stable pattern of technology use. For both of the older generations the radio was a significant medium, although it meant different things in Estonia and Sweden.

For the focus groups born in the late 1970s and the early 1990s there were less commonalities across cultures. It is quite clear that the two oldest generational cohorts came of age in a media landscape that privileged common experiences, irrespective of whether these were produced through the ideology of public service, or the ideology of state radio and television. Both of the oldest generational cohorts share memories of children's and youth programmes from the dominant mass media radio and television, but also from print media. When it came to the print media, the oldest Estonian generation shared experiences of the state-controlled youth press, while the same Swedish generational cohort emphasised comics. The contextual situation was, however, very different depending on whether they had been born during the Second World War in a country involved in the war (Estonia) or not (Sweden), and whether they had spent their formative years in the post-war situation under occupation (Estonia) or in a country where the industry was booming and the welfare system had its golden days (Sweden). This was obviously reflected in the interviews, and the cross-cultural comparison was especially fruitful when it came to the two oldest cohorts interviewed.

This does not mean that there were no common features in the focus groups of the two youngest generations. Those born in the late 1970s mentioned the news events of the murder of Olof Palme in Sweden, and the death of Leonid Brezhnev in Estonia. The interviewees in both countries also mentioned children's television programmes as a common denominator (although the specific programmes of course differed between the two cultural contexts). There were also a few common experiences among the interviewees in the early 1990s generation, which were otherwise mostly more individual memories.

For the two oldest generations, radio was the most significant medium, but, maybe a bit surprisingly, radio also seems to have been important for other generations, although in different ways. For the Swedish generations born in the late 1970s radio was the source of producing mix tapes, especially by recording hit songs from *Trackslistan* and similar music list programmes. These programmes are not children's programmes, but rather youth programmes. So, while the post-war period in Sweden saw a rise in programming for children, later generations saw the rise of youth programming.

In the interviews, the two oldest generations recalled many shared memories of the post-war and the Cold War situation, reflecting their coming of age in two different geo-political eras. The younger cohorts had fewer shared memories. The media landscape that they grew up in was more heteronomous and the historical circumstances produced few collective memories. There are some references to children's television, but whereas the Estonian focus group participants emphasised the news programme *Vremja* (in a negative way, as interrupting other, more entertaining programmes), the Swedish respondents emphasised popular culture, such as the Eurovision Song Contest. For the youngest cohort interviewed, the respondents were even more individualised in their preferences and their habits. This can partly be explained by the larger output of media platforms, and genres and content. But there are also other explanations as to why these cohorts were less coherent in their generational narrative.

One part in this generational self-understanding, and an important ingredient in the process of generationing is the nostalgic mode that members of generations give voice to in their interviews and in their accounts of past media memories. Chapter 5 discusses three types of nostalgic modes that all have a central role in the formation of the we-sense of various generations. Technostalgia is the most superficial among these (apart from quasi-nostalgic modes such as retrotyping), where remembrances of old or outdated media technologies and practices (such as letter-writing) partially revives earlier life phases. The nostalgic childhood remembrances are more passionate and are often related to children's books, indicating time irrecoverably lost. Such loss is very individual, however, and it does not contribute to the we-sense needed for a generational consciousness to develop. The nostalgia modus most important for the generational consciousness is that moment when parents realise the impossibility of transgenerational transfer of experience. This moment is definitive, cannot be remedied, and ultimately establishes the boundary between different generations.

The analysis has aimed to understand the ways in which generations are formed by way of a comparative approach, where the specific qualities of a certain generation stand out against the qualities of coevals that have had their formative years in other geo-political contexts, and where the media and historical contexts of Sweden and Estonia have been used to represent two different locations, formed by different historical unfoldings. But the comparative perspective has also been used to position generations against other generations, born at other points in time in these historical contexts (which, of course, also means that they have come of age in different media landscapes, even if within the same national setting). Empirically, this has meant analysing statistical survey data and focus group interview materials in order to identify *internal commonalities* within potential generations, as well as *external differences* regarding other preceding or succeeding generations. At the centre of such a discussion is the question of self-understanding and a sense of commonality with one's fellow generational comrades. When such commonality is acknowledged among individuals born in the same historical, geo-political and cultural position, the generation becomes actualised.

A generation as actuality, in Mannheim's sense, can be seen as an actually existing social formation, or social identity (cf. Corsten 1999: 252). Social identities, just like generations, need to have reached a correspondence between the ascribed and the self-perceived. A social identity can, for example, be ascribed to a social group by others without anyone of those within that social group being able to recognise the description. We ascribe certain traits to people and represent them with features such as gender, age, class, ethnicity, and so on. These representations do not necessarily correspond to the self-perception of these individuals. We might ascribe an upper-class position to someone (based on speech, behaviour, style, or consumption patterns), while this person might tend to perceive him- or herself as middle-class. Sociological research has, for example, shown discrepancies between objective and subjective class position (Kingston 2000), although this also varies with cultural context, for example in the United States and Sweden (Karlssson 2005). We might ascribe a particular ethnic identity, or perhaps the label 'foreigner', to someone who lives in Sweden and has dark hair, brown eyes and brown skin, while this person, based on the facts of being born in Sweden, having spent their life entirely in Sweden, having Swedish as their mother tongue, considers him or herself 'Swedish'. We might also assume, for example, that people who we meet when travelling around in Great Britain are English. However, many of them might self-identify as Welsh or Scottish. You might also assume that the person you meet in Bilbao is Spanish, while she or he might rather self-identify as Basque. And so on. The point is that if groups of people do not self-identify as belonging to a generation (or an ethnic group, or a class position), then these identities are not complete as social identities.

So, the self-perception is a founding basis of the generational identity (Aroldi 2011). Such self-perceptions do not arrive from nowhere. They are cultivated in relation to previous experience within a certain social formations and are continuously reproduced. In that reproductive process self-perceptions also become refined in the meeting between ascriptions made by others (including when the identity is challenged) and the self-perceptions of the individual as a member of a social collective. However, many perceptions are not only formed in relation to other individuals and social collectives but also in relation to media representations. This discrepancy between ascribed and self-perceived generational identity is clearly illustrated in a Swedish study of print media representations of the 'Swedish baby boomers', more commonly called 'the forties generation' (fyrtiotalisterna). In the press material that was used as a basis for the analysis, consisting of interviews with and accounts of people born in the period, the forties generation was described in two ways: those who self-identified as being a member of the forties generation emphasised their working class background, the class trajectory to the middle-class, and their hard work to achieve this position, whereas those that did not identify as belonging to the forties generation emphasised 'them' as being self-centred, spoiled and privileged (Jönsson & Jönsson 2014: 69). Such representations of these two positions towards the forties generation will by necessity have consequences for those who read and take part in them, and for the reader who was born in the 1940s these accounts will be evaluated against his or her self-perception. Reflections on one's self-perceived social or generational identity will then be triggered when one's cultural identity is challenged. On these occasions one is actively prompted to think through one's identity, and to what generation or other social or cultural formation one belongs.

A generational identity or a generational consciousness is also the basis for a generationally informed habitus (Eyerman & Turner 1998, Edmunds & Turner 2002: 13ff): that is, the bodily inscribed dispositions to act within the framework of the historical location, including the media landscape of this location, based on previous media habits and experiences. This habitus is revealed in certain situations, especially as a form of anxiety or unease in relation to novelties. Take television advertising as an example. Swedish generations born in the 1940s or earlier came of age in an advertising-free public service television landscape. When commercial breaks were introduced on the commercial television channels with the re-regulation of Swedish broadcasting in the early 1990s, this produced such unease among certain older viewers that they had to physically leave the room. Their generationally formed habitus literally prevented them from watching the commercials, whereas they were less sensitive to product placement in programmes (Bolin & Forsman 2002: 210 and 273). The generationally formed habitus includes a certain disposition among generation members, a distinct expression of the 'structure of feeling' characteristic for a specific epoch, and represents a 'natural view of the world' (Mannheim 1928/1952: 299) which privilege certain approaches to that world.

According to Mannheim (1928/1952: 292) 'members of any one generation can participate only in a temporally limited section of the historical process'. This is of course true as far as it relates to first-hand experiences. However, experience can at times be extended via mediated narratives. Take the moon landing, for example. This 'small step for a man, one giant leap for mankind' was an international news story widely reported in national media all over the word, including television. Ingrid Volkmer (2006b: 261) even views the moon landing as a 'generation-defining event' for the generation that she and her colleagues label the 'black-and-white television generation' (born between 1954 and 1959). Several of the participants in the Swedish focus group born between 1962 and 1964 had vivid memories of this event, which was broadcast live in Sweden just as in many other countries around the world, even if they also on second thought (triggered by the interview situation) realised that their memories might stem from reruns and broadcasts after the event. In this way the mediated experience contributes to the common generational we-sense – at least among the focus group participants. Thus, with the media, a specific 'section of the historical process' can be extended to include also 'prosthetic' memories (Landsberg 1995) that unite groups of people. Media events such as these, that is, events of international magnitude reported in the news media, are the fodder for such points of establishing a generational consciousness. This goes especially for those events that have ceremonial qualities, such as the moon landing, which has imprinted itself as a decisive moment in the process of history, and an event that is repeatedly mentioned in accounts by media users, not only in Sweden (see also examples in Höijer 1998: 204), but also in countries such as Australia, Austria, Germany, India, Japan and – quite naturally – the United States (Volkmer 2006a).

Mannheim emphasised the social bonds between people born at the same location in the historical process. This specific, historically constituted space and this social belonging are not enough, however, and have to be realised in experience to become a generation as actuality, through direct social interaction or via the media. Mannheim's original formulation for generation as actuality is 'Generationszusammenhang'. However, the English translation 'actuality' does not fully capture the semantic meaning of the German concept and, as Michael Corsten has pointed out, the 'difficulty in understanding "generation as actuality" derives from the vague meaning of the original German term' (Corsten 2011: 40). With the help of Merriam-Webster's dictionary, he argues that it should be viewed as 'a state of cohering' that integrates 'individuals', 'groups' (or generation units) and their respective 'meaningful experiences' (pp. 40f). In other instances he has translated it as 'generational context' (Corsten 1999: 254), and elaborated on the translation from German to English: 'Individuals of the same age, they were and are, however, only *united* [connected, German: *verbunden*] as an actual generation [*Generationszusammenhang*: coherence of generation]' (Corsten 1999: 269).

Another translational difficulty related to generation as actuality lies in the German concept of 'Schicksal', which has been translated as 'destiny' in the English version of Mannheim's text, and thus has been somewhat reduced in its original meaning. The full quote when Mannheim establishes the distinction between generation as location and actuality reads as follows:

> In order to share the same generation location, i.e. in order to be able passively to undergo or actively to use the handicaps and privileges inherent in a generation location, one must be born within the same historical and cultural region. Generation as an actuality, however, involves even more than mere co-presence in such a historical and social region. A further concrete nexus is needed to constitute generation as an actuality. This additional nexus

may be described as participation in the common destiny of this historical and social unit.

(Mannheim 1928/1952: 303)

This should be compared with the original German quote of this passage:

Man muß im selben historisch-sozialen Raume – in derselben historischen Lebensgemeinschaft – zur selben Zeit geboren worden sein, um ihr zurechenbar zu sein, um die Hemmungen und die Chancen jener Lagerung passiv ertragen, aber auch aktiv nützen zu können. Nun ist aber der Generationszusammenhang noch mehr als die so umschriebene bloße Präsenz in einer bestimmten historisch-sozialen Einheit. Irgendeine konkrete Verbindung muß noch hinzukommen, um von einem Generationszusammenhang sprechen zu können. Diese Verbundenheit könnte man kurzweg eine *Partizipation an den gemeinsamen Schicksalen* dieser historisch-sozialen Einheit bezeichnen.

(Mannheim 1928: 309, emphasis in original)

The German concept of 'Schicksalen' has a double meaning that is lost when it is translated as 'destiny', and the phenomenological dimension that the original German term carries becomes lost in the English translation (a footnote to this passage also refers back to a quote by Heidegger earlier in the text, further anchoring the phenomenological connection). The English concept of destiny is more fatalistic than the German concept (although it can have that fatalistic meaning as well).[1] But the German concept Schicksalen (similar to the corresponding Swedish concept of 'öde') can also point to the different contexts and situations that you have encountered during the course of your life and that have contributed to who you are as a person. This is very far from being a determined destiny, and points more to the aggregated experiences you have collected during your life. In Mannheim's discussion, this is used to describe the collective experiences of coevals who have, as a potential generation, accumulated a certain combination of experiences related to the context of a structure of historical events, and in certain instances can come together and act on the basis of these experiences and thus become 'actualised'.

Since the concepts of Schicksalen and Generationszusamenhang point to experiences accumulated over time, to the features that make a generational location (as a potentiality) become an actualised generation, it follows that a generation's destiny is not determined. Instead generations are dynamically *coming into being* in a process of generationing.

Generationing as a process of becoming

As history unfolds, people born at approximately the same time are exposed to events (including media events) and circumstances in the surrounding society. Media events such as the moon landing, together with other international news events (the attack on the Twin Towers in New York, the assassination of John Kennedy, the fall of the Berlin Wall, the death of Princess Diana, etc.), and more nationally delimited news events (spectacular crimes, natural disasters, but also major national sports achievements), are also events that have lived on in the media long after the date that they were first being reported. Through repetition and reruns on radio and television they become part of a general, sometimes nostalgically tainted, generational consciousness that is enhanced on every occasion that the event is retold (or rerun). Through that process they also become defining features for a generation as actuality.

Together with the self-perceptions and the ascriptions described in the previous section, including those in the mass media, these repeated accounts of the significant news moments are important components in the process of generationing (Siibak & Vittadini 2012, Siibak et al. 2014). Generationing as a process implies that people are not destined to be specific generations by birth, but that certain cohorts over time receive a generational consciousness and self-understanding that make them understand themselves as members of a specific generation. And the media are an important factor in this becoming. The concept of generationing, as picked up from child culture research (Alanen 2001) and adopted by Nicoletta Vittadini, Andra Siibak and others (Siibak & Vittadini 2012, Vittadini et al. 2013b, McDaniel 2004) has been used to point to such a process of becoming, where different cohorts 'interdependently construct each other by purifying their distinctive sets of practices' (Vittadini et al. 2013b: 66). In the next few paragraphs I will try to further develop that conceptualisation by discussing two features that are foundational to such practices. These are, on the one hand, *memory formation*, and, on the other hand, what could be called the *generational narrative*. Both memory formation and narrative construction are temporal features with specific dynamics of their own.

When it comes to memory formation there is a certain social and mediatised constitution of the past that impacts on the way in which generations are formed and developed. The scholarly study of how people remember episodes, events or past experiences is of course enormous, but in this specific context the most important part is research into collective memory formation, that is, those memories that give 'greater emphasis to the social context than to autobiographical, personal memory' (Teer-Tomaselli 2006: 225). The bottom line, however, is that collective memories are produced by individual subjects, and to these individuals the memories will be perceived as personal. As Birgitta Höijer (1998: 28ff) has pointed out, personal memories are of several kinds: memories of specific events, generalised memories, factual memories and memories related to one's own identity. Memories of *specific events* are often accounted for in interviews in very precise ways, often detailed and exact in their descriptions of time and place, as well as detailed in the description of the emotional state connected to the event. Typically this concerns memories of dramatic news events that have stood out against the ordinary flow of everyday happenings. Many accounts of media use and habit are, however, in the form of *generalised memories* that deal with how things were more generally, for example that one used to listen to Radio Luxembourg in the evenings, but where the experience of each individual evening is less important. *Factual memories* are often related to specific factual circumstances, such as the brand of the radio transmitter ('it was a beautiful and expensive German radio', as an interviewee in the oldest Estonian focus group remembered). Lastly, *memories related to one's own identity* can, of course, refer to the personal identity (how one was at a certain point in time) or to the collective identity (how we were, or how we came to be the persons we are now). In the process of memory formation, and in the interview situation, such memories take narrative form. When asked about one's early memories, one tends to contextualise habits and behaviour into coherent stories. This is not only to please a focus group moderator in the specific interview situation, but also in order to make the memories make sense to oneself. Such memory work also tends to produce an increasing amount of narrative coherence in the stories over time.

One example of this is the account given by Mare in the previous chapter of how she was given the book *Pöial-Liisi* by her aunt while hospitalised with diphtheria at the age of four. This prosthetic memory is in a way factual, since we get a lot of detail about the book and its cover, but it is also obviously the result of a narrative related to Mare's personal experience of diphtheria. It is thus woven into her life-story, where it is given prominence as a distinct experience from her childhood years. In a similar way we can also see traces of such narrativisation in the story about the death of Soviet leader Leonid Brezhnev, which was recalled by two of the participants in the Estonian focus group born in the late 1970s. As his recollection reveals, the memory is a product of family history, and particularly what had been recounted by his mother ('mum has told me').

The story about *Pöial-Liisi* obviously relates to an individual and personal memory, and the nostalgic account that it represents does not connect to the experiences of the other focus group participants, and is hence not part of any collective memory. On the other hand, the story told about the death of Brezhnev, and how this event led to the cancelling of children's television programmes for several days *does* connect to others in the focus group, and is clearly a focal point for the construction of a generational experience that goes beyond the individual. Furthermore, it also involves several different generations because it is the respondent's mother who is the reference point for the story and who is referred to as a verification of its accuracy. It is thus both a personal and a generalised memory, and we can suspect that Andres's exclamation – 'A day off school!' – is more of a generalised memory pointing to his knowledge of how things used to be at times of national mourning than it is a memory of this specific event. Again, this would confirm its status as part of a generational narrative alluding to the generational experience of having grown up in the Soviet Union, and the specific ways in which the media worked in those days.

From the above we can see how generations develop and become more homogeneous over the years with the help of small anecdotes that other coevals can recognise themselves in. In fact, one could argue that generations come into being through narration. This means that the memories among younger generations should be expected to be relatively heterogeneous, something that is also pointed out in previous research (e.g. Volkmer 2006a). As time goes by some of the individual and less common traits will fade into oblivion (or become marginalised), while those memories and experiences that take the form of recognisable stories will resonate with a common experiential structure (habitus), and eventually the stories will be part of a larger generational narrative. Such narratives will gradually help build and construct the generational 'we-sense' where a specific 'generational discourse' emerges (Boccia Artieri 2011: 110). This means that it is harder for young generations to self-identify as a generation because the generational narrative has not yet been developed and refined in a master discourse around which the generational 'we' is formed.

This means that the cohort born in the 1940s have had a longer time to develop a generational identity when compared to the cohort born in the early 1990s. The fact that the 'baby boomers' have received such an amount of attention should be taken as an indicator of that generation's importance, but the attention in itself is also part of the construction of the generational narrative and becomes a self-fulfilling, prescriptive manual for this generation. This manual includes both the shared memories, the nostalgic features that circulate among coevals, *and* the narratives of popular culture – the reruns of *Woodstock* (1970), the cults of the Beatles and the Rolling Stones – as well as the academic analyses of that generation. Taken together, the discursive repository of generation markers is part of the construction of the self-perception of this generation. In this construction, the media and culture industries indeed play an active part through the provision of media representations, but also as mediators of collective memories, producing a 'generational semantics' (Corsten 1999: 260ff) consisting of 'interpretive models, evaluation principles and linguistic devices through which shared experience is transformed in discourse within the forms of daily interaction' (Aroldi 2011: 54).

The linguistic forms of interaction and the 'generational semantics' also point to the *role of language and communication* in the formation of generational narratives and in generationing (Opermann 2013). Linguistic communication is an important feature in the construction of a generational we-sense, not least since a generational consciousness can only be conceptualised in language. Language has also been a central feature in the theory of generations, including Mannheim (1928/1952), and Gumpert and Cathcart (1985), but also among those interested in memory formation such as Halbwachs (1992), who held that collective memory could only be formed and 'reconstructed' within the frameworks of a common language. However, whereas Halbwachs discusses the reconstruction of collective memories in language, Mannheim, and Gumpert and Cathcart use language more as a metaphor and an analogy for the development of a generational consciousness and disposition for producing a 'natural view of the world' (Mannheim 1928/1952: 299).

Such a natural view of the world includes a certain disposition that is embedded within the potential generations located in specific media and social landscapes. It is activated in certain instances or *moments*, surfaces and is made the object for reflection. This can be seen in an interview situation discussing the media use of other generations (parents, children), but can also be prompted by fictional accounts or when one recognises oneself in a blog posting or in conversations in everyday social life. These moments are the building bricks in the process of generationing and, through continuous repetition, they slowly build the generational consciousness and inform the habitus.

The rhythm of ages – mediatisation and historical change

The idea of generations, argues Paul Ricoeur, 'expresses several brute facts about human biology', and 'the average age of procreation' (Ricoeur 1985/1990: 110). Such biological facts relate mainly to the generational succession order, and although these facts actualise and provoke reflections on human existence in the sense that we all know that we one day will die, while our children, or even more so children in general, will succeed us, this fact alone does not automatically produce social solidarity with, or understanding of, coevals. Of course, we might sometimes discuss with our friends of the same age the relation to our parents, or we might discuss the troubles we have in raising our children together with other parents in a way that binds us together. But that bond will only last for that single moment, since it only concerns these 'brute facts' of kinship relations. In a pre-modern world where each cohort could be expected to lead a life almost identical to the previous cohort, these 'brute facts' are the only ones important for the generational consciousness, which suggests that this 'consciousness' will be rather restricted. This means that the most relevant generational relation for pre-industrial eras was the *vertical* dimension of generation as kinship. This generational concept is vertical in the sense that what is important is the succession order. In its modern (post-industrial) form the concept takes on another meaning, adding a *horizontal* dimension of coevals that share a similar location in the historical process and can draw on experiences that previous generations cannot. Such a horizontal connection can be actualised through the common nostalgia produced when people realise the impossibility of transferring experience across to succeeding generations, as was exemplified in Chapter 5.

As Gumpert and Cathcart (1985) point out in relation to the media, the Industrial Revolution and the increased speed at which new technologies more generally replace older ones in a specific technological rhythm should provoke a certain sentiment related to modernity and the process of modernisation that actualises self-reflection and an experience of perpetual change. This sentiment would then presumably produce social solidarity with coevals in the same social situation. Technological rhythms are of course far from regular, and the depth of the technological waves also runs shallow at some times and deeper at others.

Furthermore, as more and more societal technologies are today media technologies of one sort or another, the media could be supposed to have an increasingly central position in the formation of this solidarity. This solidarity, however, would then need to take a discursive form in order for it to circulate among individual members of society. It would have to be narrated, retold, and its experience formulated and related to social others, who could on the one hand be coevals, but could also be preceding or succeeding generations.

The discourse on perpetual change and the idea of there being increasingly shorter time spans between technological revolutions is common in the social sciences and the humanities, and some would argue that modern society is characterised by 'social acceleration' (Rosa 2005/2013), where the exchanges of technology appear at increasingly short intervals. Increased speed of technological change would then, presumably, produce shorter generational spans and a faster social rhythm due to technological change. In popular discourse this, of course, produces ever new generational concepts (Generations x, y, z and so on), but there is very little empirical evidence to back up such claims beyond the marketing jargon of what could be called the agents of the audience industry: that is, those who make their living from trying to persuade producers of consumer products and services that they can reach new, unexploited market segments (Helsper & Eynon 2010, Hargittai 2010). In addition, Mannheim reflected on 'the accelerated pace of social change characteristic of our time' (Mannheim 1928/1952: 287). In fact, this is one of the more characteristic motivations for doing social research, and as I have argued elsewhere we find this idea appearing continuously over the twentieth century (Bolin 2011: 11). In fact, one could argue that the notion of living in times of constant change is the founding experience of modernity (cf. Berman 1982/1988). The rhythm of collective, social life, however, which is arrhythmic along diversities in the combination of life course, age and generational factors, seems to prevent an increased speed in 'generational turnover', irrespective of the speed of 'technological turnover'.

The idea of a recurring interval for generational succession has been the basis for many who have theorised generations. José Ortega y Gasset (1923/1931) and his student Julián Marías (1961/1970) argued that generational exchanges follow a law-like rhythm. Wilhelm Pinder (1926) tried to find the measure of artistic generations, and William Strauss and Neil Howe (1991), in their attempt to systematise American generations from 1584 and onwards, sought to find a systematic pulse-rate to generational cycles. Mannheim explicitly rejects the idea of a law-like rhythm, since '[a]ny biological rhythm must work itself out through the medium of social events' (Mannheim 1928/1952: 286); and indeed, Mannheim's initial criticism of 'the positivist formulation of the problem' is because of its mechanistic dismissal of the social (cf. Pilcher 1994: 484ff). However, Mannheim, like Ricoeur, does not deny the biological dimension in the generational process. They rather point to the necessity of complementing the biological with the social and the experiential. The rhythm of experience can only occur in the self-perception of individuals, faced with the 'brute facts' of life as biologically constituted – 'birth, aging, death' (Ricoeur 1985/1990: 110). In that sense the biological rhythm of 'contemporaries, predecessors, and successors' is just the biological context that adds to the technological, geo-political and social setting and produces what Ricoeur, in reference to Alfred Schutz (1967), calls 'a community of time', a specific space where people are 'growing old together' (Ricoeur 1985/1990: 113).

With Ricoeur and Mannheim we can then think of the analytical perspective of generation as a social theory of time, whereby individuals and groups are located in the historical process, but where they also actively impact on that process. This also means that Mannheim's theory of generations, and other theorists following in his tradition, emphasise historical change (as compared with a functionalist analysis that focuses on stability and reproduction; cf. Eisenstedt 1956). Historical change is in Mannheim's theory brought on by social relations between generations. However, as has been exemplified in the analytical chapters, there are also cultural features that are significant for historical change, many of which are related to media, both as technologies and as structures of content. The next section will discuss the relationship between cultural and historical change and the process of mediatisation, and the extent to which the media are important enough to merit a concept of media generations.

Mediatisation and media generations

If the media are important features in the formation of the generational identity, and thus for historical and cultural change, then the character of the process of mediatisation would also be an important context. In the digital era of ubiquitous and seemingly endless access to archived media texts, it was easy to forget how time-bound the past pleasures connected to the screen media of film and television have been, and how transient the experience of different stars in different periods of the twentieth century has been. The experience of Hollywood stars in specific films lasted for as long as the films featured in theatres, and the television and radio personalities were even more transient, since there was no option to go and see the TV programme a second time as one could with a cinematic screening. Only music stars lived on through the medium of the gramophone. In fact, it was through non-transient media with archival qualities – such as the gramophone and, of course, already previously with the book medium, but later with the magnetic tape and the video cassette player – that the transient quality of the mass media could be overcome. It is important to note that the question of whether there were media generations or not only appeared following the introduction of the plurality of media technologies following the rise and spread of television.

So, do *media generations* exist? This is the question that a book with the title *Media Generations* should be able to answer. The short answer is Yes – and No. Which one is preferred will depend on what one means by 'the media' and what approach one has to the mediatisation process. The institutional perspective on mediatisation is not really helpful here because it mainly deals with the role of media as institutions and their impact on other societal institutions – most often how the institution of journalism affects political institutions. The technological perspective would, in this respect, seemingly have more to offer in terms of impact on the generational consciousness because this perspective focuses on the ways in which technology impacts on mental structures and conceptions. Marshall McLuhan's main point, for example, was that electronic media changed people's perceptions of the world. McLuhan's opening paragraph of *Understanding Media: The Extensions of Man* is telling in this context:

> After three thousand years of explosion, by means of fragmentary and mechanical technologies, the Western world is imploding. During the mechanical ages we had extended our bodies in space. Today, after more than a century

of electric technology, we have extended our central nervous system itself in a global embrace, abolishing both space and time as far as our planet is concerned. Rapidly, we approach the final phase of the extensions of man—the technological simulation of consciousness, when the creative process of knowing will be collectively and corporately extended to the whole of human society, much as we have already extended our senses and our nerves by the various media.

(McLuhan 1964: 3)

If what McLuhan describes as the results of changes in the way in which people learn things, and the media is the cause of these changes, then it would not be unreasonable to talk about media generations. However, this would not be the 'radio generation', or even the 'TV generation', but the generational consciousness formed by the totality of the electronic media landscape, including the telegraph, the telephone, the gramophone, the radio and television taken together. Rather than being influenced by any single medium, this would be *an influence of the totality of the media landscape as such*.

Chapters 2 and 3 gave some examples of media user patterns of different cohorts. From these examples (Figures 2.1 and 3.2), we can see that generations born in the early 1950s have a user pattern of the functions on the mobile closer to the cohort born in the early 1980s, compared to the cohort born in the early 1930s, despite the fact that the early 1950s cohort was born only twenty years after the early 1930s cohort but thirty years before the early 1980s cohort. Signe Opermann (2014) came to the same conclusion in her study of news media generations in Estonia (from where Table 2.1 is borrowed). It is also in line with the findings of Andreas Hepp and his colleagues, who, based on qualitative interviews with German media users, make a division between the traditional 'mass media generation', the 'digital generation', and in-between these, the 'sandwich generation' (Hepp 2014: 30f). This generation is similar to the one that Opermann following Pilcher (1994) calls an 'intermediary or buffer generation', who came of age with the traditional mass media, but during the course of their working lives have gradually incorporated digital media (Hepp, Berg & Roitsch 2015: 24).

In their analysis of German media generations Hepp and his colleagues have suggested that media generations are defined by their 'self-positioning' (Selbstpositionierung) as discursively distinguished from *other* media generations (Hepp, Berg & Roitsch 2015: 31). The previous chapters have given plenty of such examples of self-positioning, both as indirect and as direct references to other generations and to the we-sense. This self-positioning or self-understanding is also related to a media landscape in constant change. There is, however, a recurring idea that is central to that self-positioning – and that is the distinction that one makes in relation to digital media. As argued in Chapter 4, older generations also use digital media, but they have elaborate arguments for why they do not use them as much as the younger generations, or why they find the ways in which younger generations use, for example, mobile phones not suitable for themselves. Correspondingly, younger generations talk about their parents' generation as one that has not really grasped the changes.

From this we can also conclude that there are no sharp divisions between media generations, but that there are more gradual and fine-tuned differences in approach. This is also why concepts such as 'digital generations' will not adequately capture the dynamics of generational exchanges, and how generations also change internally over time. Let me return to the example with mobile phones in Figure 3.2 above, and how the uses of this device have changed over the past decade. As can be seen from the figure, media use within the same cohort is not static, irrespective of which cohort we look at. Also the older generation – what Hepp et al. (2014) would call the mass media generation – does change its behaviour and incorporate new ways of using the mobile. But they do so with a temporal lag, and not as intensely as the younger generations.

This is also why it is more appropriate to view the mediatisation process as a dynamic force that gradually affects media user behaviour. There are no sharp brakes introduced by new media technologies or content, but a slow 'moulding' of everyday media use, to use another of Hepp's (2013) metaphors. This is more in line with a view of mediatisation as a 'meta-process' that does not have immediate causal effects, as is suggested in some mediatisation theory, but a view on mediatisation as an integrated part of wider social and cultural processes (Krotz 2007). And if media are an important part of such wider processes, then it would be unreasonable to hold that the media are not a significant part of the generational experience.

The generational consciousness, however, is not something we go around and actively contemplate all the time. As with other meta-processes, such as individualisation and globalisation, this process is deeply embedded in our experience, and is only activated in certain situations – just as we can realise at times that our individualised behaviour differs from that of others, or that something related to our work is suddenly affected by the meta-process of globalisation. But it is in such situations that a generation becomes 'actual', and the generational context (zusammenhang) manifests itself. The generational identity is for most of the time hibernating, and is only activated in those specific moments. This also goes for the media generational consciousness. Most often we do not think of our own relation to the media, they are like air to us (Deuze 2012), but in certain situations the media context of our past is brought back to us – a class reunion; a visit to a concert with past musical heroes; a revisit to a cherished childhood film; or the discovery of the old family album in the attic – and we can then connect it to other media contexts, related to other generational formations. We might do this in relation to generalised others, across cultures, across time, but we can also do this in relation to specific others – people who are representatives of kinship generations that can be presumed to have had other experiences than our own.

Final words

Kinship binds family histories together diachronically, whereas generation as a social formation binds coevals together through synchronic relationships. My mother was, just as I was, born in Stockholm. My grandmother Dagny and my grandfather

Evert, however, were born in the north of Sweden. They both moved to Stockholm in their late teens to find work, whereas my great-grandmother, who was also born in the north of Sweden, never moved from the local environment where she was born and raised. We all share the same family history, however, and are thus part of the generational succession order. But we do not share the same experiences, since our lives have been formed by strikingly different contexts: socially, economically and culturally. The photo was taken in 1939, and my great grandmother was 61 years old at the time. By today's standards, she looks older, but the living conditions, as well as having given birth to thirteen children, have marked her body. She would live for another 25 years after this occasion, until 1964, and I remember her from my early youth as a very old woman, sitting in the corner at family gatherings.

To be born and raised as I was, during the height of the Swedish welfare state, is socially very far removed from the rural environment and the hardships that followed from that peasantry and forestry in which my great grandmother grew up. Although my mother and myself were both born in Stockholm, we are worlds apart when it comes to our individual experiences, including media experiences. Today, I live just one block away from the house in which my mother was born in 1933, and a few blocks from the cinema where she went to watch *Snow White* in 1938. There are no longer any cinema theatres along Hornsgatan, the main street that cuts across the island of Södermalm, which is the largest of the inner city islands on which Stockholm is built. And if there was one, it would probably be a multi-screen cinema that would make the experience different anyway. My children have played in the same park as she did. Or, more correctly, the park might have the same geographical coordinates, but the 60–70 years that have passed since my mother played there make it a fundamentally different place. Nonetheless, our family is bound together over time, diachronically, across the ages. As individuals in the generational succession order, however, each member in this order is also part of a synchronic bond with his or her social generation. At the intersection of these experiences and the actions that they privilege is produced 'the rhythm of ages'.

Note

1 I would like to thank Andreas Hepp for discussions on the subtleties of the German language related to the concept of Schicksalen.

REFERENCES

Adams, Ann Jensen (1994): 'Seventeenth-century Dutch Landscape Painting', in W.J. Thomas Mitchell (ed.): *Landscape and Power*, Chicago: Chicago University Press, 35–76.

Åker, Patrik (2015): 'The Space Race in the Swedish Press during the Cold War Era: A Celebration of Transparent Western Television', in Hanrik G. Bastiansen and Rolf Werenskjold (eds): *The Nordic Media and the Cold War*. Göteborg: Nordicom, 147–65.

Alanen, Leena (2001): 'Childhood as Generational Condition: Children's Daily Lives in a Central Finland Town', in Leena Alanen and Barry Mayall (eds): *Conceptualizing Child–Adult Relations*. London: Routledge, 129–143.

Altheide, David L. and Robert P. Snow (1979): *Media Logic*. Beverly Hills: Sage.

Altheide, David L. and Robert P. Snow (1991): *Media Worlds in the Postjournalism Era*. New York: Aldine de Gruyter.

Ang, Ien (1985/1991): *Watching Dallas. Soap Opera and the Melodramatic Imagination*. London & New York: Routledge.

Aristotle (1997): *Metaphysics* (a revised text with introduction and commentary by W.D. Ross). Oxford: Clarendon.

Aroldi, Piermarco (2011): 'Generational Belonging Between Media Audiences and ICT Users', in Fausto Colombo and Leopoldina Fortunati (eds): *Broadband Society and Generational Changes*. Frankfurt am Main: Peter Lang, 51–67.

Aroldi, Piermarco and Fausto Colombo (2013): 'Questioning "Digital Global Generations". A Critical Approach'. *Northern Lights,* 11(1): 175–190.

Aroldi, Piermarco and Cristina Ponte (2012): 'Adolescents of the 1960s and 1970s: An Italian-Portuguese Comparison between Two Generations of Audiences'. *Cyberpsychology: Journal of Psychosocial Research on Cyberspace*, 6:2. Available at www.cyberpsychology.eu/view.php?cisloclanku=2012081004&article=3. Last accessed 25 December 2013.

Åström, Lissie (1986): *I kvinnoled. Om kvinnors liv genom tre generationer*. Malmö: Liber.

Åström, Lissie (1990): *Fäder och söner. Bland svenska män i tre generationer*. Stockholm: Carlssons.

Baron, Naomi S. (2010): 'Introduction to Special Section: Mobile Phones in Cross-Cultural Context: Sweden, Estonia, the USA and Japan'. *New Media & Society,* 12(1): 3–11.

Baron, Naomi S. and Ylva Hård af Segerstad (2010): 'Cross-Cultural Patterns in Mobile Phone Use: Public Space and Reachability in Sweden, USA and Japan'. *New Media & Society,* 12(1): 13–34.

Baudrillard, Jean (1971): 'Requiem pour les Media'. *Utopie*, 4: 35–51.

Baudrillard, Jean (1983): *Simulations*. New York: Semiotext(e).

Becker, Karin, Jan Ekecrantz and Tom Olsson (2000): 'Picturing Politics in 20th Century Sweden', in Karin Becker, Jan Ekecrantz and Tom Olsson (eds): *Picturing Politics. Visual and Textual Formations of Modernity in the Swedish Press*. Stockholm: JMK, 8–25.

Bengtsson, Stina and Lars Lundgren (2005): *The Don Quixote of Youth Culture: Media Use and Cultural Preferences among Students in Estonia and Sweden*. Huddinge: Södertörn Academic Studies.

Benjamin, Walter (1936/1977), 'The Work of Art in the Age of Mechanical Reproduction', in James Curran, Michael Gurevitch and Janet Wollacott (eds) *Mass Communication and Society*. London: Edward Arnold, 384–408.

Benjamin, Walter (1955/1999): 'Thesis on the Philosophy of History', in Hanna Arendt (ed.): *Illuminations*. London: Pimlico.

Bergström, Annika (2005): 'Den fjärde vågen', in Sören Holmberg and Lennart Weibull (eds): *Lyckan kommer, lyckan går*. Göteborg: SOM Institute, 363–72.

Berman, Marshall (1982/1988): *All That Is Solid Melts Into Air. The Experience of Modernity*. New York: Penguin.

Berntsen, Dorthe and David C. Rubin (2002): 'Emotionally Charged Autobiographical Memories Across the Life Span: The Recall of Happy, Sad, Traumatic, and Involuntary Memories'. *Psychology and Aging*, 17(4): 636–52.

Bijsterveld, Karin and José van Dijck (eds) (2009): *Sound Souvenirs: Audio Technologies, Memory and Cultural Practices*. Amsterdam: Amsterdam University Press.

Björkin, Mats (2015): 'Reconstructing Past Media Ecologies: The 1960s Generation in Sweden'. *European Journal of Communication*, 30(1): 50–63.

Bjur, Jakob (2009): *Transforming Audiences: Patterns of Individualization in Television Viewing*. Göteborg: JMG.

Blumler, Jay G., Jack M. McLeod and Karl Erik Rosengren (eds) (1992): *Comparatively Speaking: Communication and Culture Across Space and Time*. Newbury Park: Sage.

BMF (1994): *Estonian Media Book '94*. Tallinn: Baltic Media Facts/Digipress Est/Viestinnäntekijät.

Boccia Artieri, Giovanni (2011): 'Generational "We Sense" in the Networked Space: User Generated Representation of the Youngest Generation', in Fausto Colombo and Leopoldina Fortunati (eds); *Broadband Society and Generational Changes*. Frankfurt am Main: Peter Lang, 109–20.

Boettiger, Henry M. (1977): 'Our Sixth-and-a-Half Sense', in Ithiel de Sola Pool (ed.): *The Social Impact of the Telephone*. Cambridge, MA.: MIT Press.

Bolin, Göran (1994): 'Beware! Rubbish! Popular Culture and Strategies of Distinction'. *Young*, 2(1): 33–49.

Bolin, Göran (1997): 'Postvideogenerationen. Ålders- och generationsidentitet bland filmbytande unga män'. *Filmhäftet*, 97–98: 71–81.

Bolin, Göran (2003): *Variations, Media Landscapes, History. Frameworks for an Analysis of Contemporary Media Landscapes*. Huddinge: Södertörn University.

Bolin, Göran (2004): 'Research on Youth and Youth Cultures'. *Young*, 12(3): 237–43.

Bolin, Göran (2006a): 'Makten over tekniken eller teknikens makt? Mönster i mobilanvändning 2005', in Sören Holmberg and Lennart Weibull (eds): *Du stora nya värld*. Göteborg: SOM-Institutet, 403–12.

Bolin, Göran (2006b): 'Electronic Geographies. Media Landscapes as Technological and Symbolic Environments', in Jesper Falkheimer and André Jansson (eds): *Geographies of Communication. The Spatial Turn in Media Studies*. Göteborg: Nordicom, 67–86.

Bolin, Göran (2010): 'Domesticating the Mobile in Estonia'. *New Media & Society*, 12(1): 55–73.

Bolin, Göran (2011): *Value and the Media. Cultural Production and Consumption in Digital Markets*. Farnham: Ashgate.

Bolin, Göran (2014a): 'Generationsskiftningar i mobillandskapet', in Lennart Weibull, Henrik Oscarsson and Annika Bergström (eds): *Mittfåra & marginal*, Göteborg: SOM-Institutet, 229–37.

Bolin, Göran (2014b): 'Institution, Technology, World: Relationships between the Media, Culture and Society', in Knut Lundby (ed.): *Mediatization of Communication*, Berlin & Boston: De Gruyter Mouton, 175–97.

Bolin, Göran (2014c): 'Media Generations: Objective and Subjective Media Landscapes and Nostalgia among Generations of Media Users'. *Participations,* 11(2): 108–31.

Bolin, Göran and Jonas Andersson Schwarz (2015): 'Heuristics of the Algorithm. Big Data, User Interpretation and Institutional Translation'. *Big Data and Society*, 2(2): 1–12.

Bolin, Göran and Michael Forsman (2002): *Bingolotto: Produktion, text, reception*. Huddinge: Södertörn University.

Bolin, Göran and Eli Skogerbø (2013): 'Age, Generation and the Media'. *Northern Lights*, 11(1): 3–14.

Bolin, Göran and Oscar Westlund (2009): 'Mobile Generations. The Role of the Mobile in the Shaping of Swedish Media Generations'. *International Journal of Communication*, 3: 108–24.

Bourdieu, Pierre (1972/1977): *Outline of a Theory of Practice*. Cambridge: Cambridge University Press.

Bourdieu, Pierre (1983): 'The Field of Cultural Production, Or: The Economic World Reversed'. *Poetics,* 12: 311–56.

Bourdieu, Pierre (1984/1990): *Homo Academicus*. Cambridge: Polity.

Bourdieu, Pierre (1989): 'Social Space and Symbolic Power'. *Sociological Theory*, 7(1): 14–25.

Bourdieu, Pierre (1990): *In Other Words. Essays Towards a Reflexive Sociology*. Cambridge: Polity.

Bourdieu, Pierre (1992/1996): *The Rules of Art. Genesis and Structure of the Literary Field*. Cambridge: Polity.

Boym, Svetlana (2001): *The Future of Nostalgia*. New York: Basic Books.

Bristow, Jennie (2015): *Baby Boomers and Generational Conflict*. Basingstoke: Palgrave Macmillan.

Brown, Raymond E. (1994): *The Death of the Messiah: From Gethsemane to the Grave. A Commentary on the Passion Narratives in the Four Gospels* (two volumes). New York: Doubleday.

Brunsdon, Charlotte (1991): 'Satellite Dishes and the Landscapes of Taste'. *New Formations*, 15: 23–40.

Buckingham, David and Rebekah Willett (eds) (2006): *Digital Generations. Children, Young People, and New Media*. Mahwah, NJ: Lawrence Erlbaum Associates.

Bude, Heinz (1997): 'Die "Wir-Schicht" der Generation'. *Berliner Journal für Soziologie*, 7(2): 197–204.

Burnett, Judith (2010): *Generations. The Time Machine in Theory and Practice*. Farnham: Ashgate.

Campbell, Scott W. (2007): 'A Cross-Cultural Comparison of Perceptions and Uses of Mobile Telephony'. *New Media & Society*, 9(2): 343–63.

Carey, James (1981): 'McLuhan and Mumford: The Roots of Modern Media Analysis'. *Journal of Communication*, 31(3): 162–78.

Carlsson, Ulla and Ulrika Facht (2007): *MedieSverige 2007*. Göteborg: Nordicom.

Casey, Edward S. (2004): 'Mapping the World in Works of Art', in Bruce V. Folz and Robert Frodeman (eds): *Rethinking Nature. Essays in Environmental Philosophy*. Bloomington & Indianapolis: Indiana University Press, 260–9.

Castells, Manuel, Mireia Fernández-Ardèvol, Jack Linchuan Qui and Araba Sey (2007): *Mobile Communication and Society. A Global Perspective*. Cambridge: MIT Press.

Chisholm, Lynne (1995): 'European Youth Research: Tour de Force or Turmbauzu Babel?', in Lynne Chisholm, Peter Buchner, Heinz-Hermann Krüger and Manuela Bois-Reymond (eds): *Growing up in Europe: Contemporary Horizons in Childhood and Youth Studies*. Berlin: Walter de Gruyter, 21–32.

Cola, Marta (2014): 'Theoretical Approach to Generational Belonging between Media Use and Migratory Background'. Paper presented at the conference 'The Future of Audience Research: Agenda, Theory and Social Significance, Ljubljana 5-7 February 2014.

Colombo, Fausto (2011): 'The Long Wave of Generations', in Fausto Colombo and Leopoldina Fortunati (eds): *Broadband Society and Generational Changes*. Frankfurt am Main: Peter Lang, 19–35.

Colombo, Fausto and Leopoldina Fortunati (eds) (2011): *Broadband Society and Generational Changes*. Frankfurt am Main: Peter Lang.

Corsten, Michael (1999): 'The Time of Generations'. *Time & Society*, 8(2): 249–72.

Corsten, Michael (2011): 'Media as the "Historical New" for Young Generations', in Fausto Colombo and Leopoldina Fortunati (eds): *Broadband Society and Generational Changes*. Frankfurt am Main: Peter Lang, 37–49.

Couldry, Nick (2012): *Media, Society, World. Social Theory and Digital Media Practice*. Cambridge: Polity.

Coupland, Douglas (1991): *Generation X – Tales from an Accelerated Culture*. London: Abacus.

Crisell, Andrew (1997): *An Introductory History of British Broadcasting*. Second edition. London & New York: Routledge.

Cubitt, Sean (1991). *Timeshift. On Video Culture*. London & New York: Routledge.

Davidson, Jane W. and Sandra Garrido (2014): *My Life as a Playlist*. Crawley, WA: UWA Publishing.

Deacon, David and James Stanyer (2014): 'Mediatization: Key Concept or Conceptual Bandwagon?' *Media, Culture & Society*, 36(7): 1032–44.

Deacon, David and James Stanyer (2015): '"Mediatization *and*", or "mediatisation *of*"? A Response to Hepp et al.' *Media, Culture & Society*, 37(4): 655–7.

Deutsch, Karl (1987), 'Prologue: Achievements and Challenges in 2000 Years of Comparative Research', in Meinolf Dierkes, Hans N. Weiler and Ariane Berthoin Antal (eds): *Comparative Policy Research: Learning from Experience*. Aldershot: Gower.

Deuze, Mark (2012): *Media Life*. Cambridge: Polity.

Dhoest, Alexander (2015), 'Connections That Matter: The Relative Importance of Ethnic-cultural Origin, Age and Generation in Media Uses Among Diasporic Youth in Belgium'. *Journal of Children and Media*, Online First, DOI: 10.1080/17482798.2015.1022562.

Dhoest, Alexander, Kaarina Nikunen and Marta Cola (2013): 'Exploring Media Use among Migrant Families in Europe: Theoretical Foundations and Reflections'. *Observatorio (OBS*) Journal*, 13–31.

Doherty, Thomas (1988): *Teenagers & Teenpics. The Juvenilization of American Movies in the 1950s*. Boston: Unwin Hyman.

Edmunds, June and Bryan S. Turner (2002): *Generations, Culture and Society*. Buckingham & Philadelphia: Open University Press.

Edmunds, June and Bryan S. Turner (2005): 'Global Generations: Social Change in the Twentieth Century'. *The British Journal of Sociology*, 56(4): 559–77.

Eisenstadt, Shmuel N. (1956): *From Generation to Generation. Age Groups and Social Structure*. Chicago: Glencoe Press.

Eisenstadt, Shmuel N. (1988): 'Youth, Generational Consciousness and Historical Change', in Janusz Kuczyński, Shmuel N. Eisenstadt, Boubakar Ly and Lotika Sarkar (eds): *Perspectives on Contemporary Youth*. Hong Kong: United Nations University, 91–110.

Ekecrantz, Jan (2004): 'In Other Worlds. Mainstream Imagery of Eastern Neighbors', in Kristina Riegert (ed.): *News of the Other. Tracing Identity in Scandinavian Constructions of the Eastern Baltic Sea Region*. Göteborg: Nordicom, 43–69.

Erikson, Erik Homburger (1959): *Identity and the Life Cycle: Selected Papers*. New York: International Universities Press.

Eyerman, Ron (2002): 'Intellectuals and the Construction of an African American Identity: Outline of a Generational Approach', in June Edmunds and Bryan S. Turner (eds): *Generational Consciousness, Narrative and Politics*. Lanham, Boulder, New York & Oxford: Rowman & Littlefield, 51–74.

Eyerman, Ron and Bryan S. Turner (1998): 'Outline of a Theory of Generations'. *European Journal of Social Theory*, 1(1): 91–106.

Findahl, Olle (2013): *Svenskarna och Internet 2013*. Stockholm: Stiftelsen för Internetinfrastruktur.

Finn, Caryl (1992): *Strains of Utopia: Gender, Nostalgia and Hollywood Film Music*. Princeton, NJ: Princeton University Press.

Fornäs, Johan and Göran Bolin (eds) (1994): *Youth Culture in Late Modernity*. London, Thousand Oaks & New Delhi: Sage.

Forsman, Michael (2010): *Lokal radio i konkurrens 1975-2010. Utbud, publik och varumärken*. Stockholm: Ekerlids förlag.

Forsman, Michael and Göran Bolin (1997): 'Video', in Ulla Carlsson and Catharina Bucht (eds): *MedieSverige 1997. Statistik och analys*. Göteborg: Nordicom, 331–42.

Fortunati, Leopoldina (2011): 'Digital Native Generation and the New Media', in Fausto Colombo and Leopoldina Fortunati (eds): *Broadband Society and Generational Changes*. Frankfurt am Main: Peter Lang, 201–19.

Frith, Simon (1978): *The Sociology of Rock*. London: Constable.

Gahlin, Anders (1977), *Radio, TV och tidningar i tre generationer*. Stockholm: SR/PUB.

Garnert, Jan (2005): Hallå! Om telefonens första tid i Sverige. Lund: Historiska Media.

Gilleard, Chris and Paul Higgs (2007): 'The Third Age and the Baby Boomers: Two Approaches to the Structuring of Later Life'. *International Journal of Ageing and Later Life*, 2(2): 13–30.

Gillis, John R. (1974): *Youth and History: Tradition and Change in European Age Relations 1770–present*. San Diego & London: Academic Press.

Gumpert, Gary and Robert Cathcart (1985): 'Media Grammars, Generations and Media Gaps'. *Critical Studies in Mass Communication*, 2(1): 23–35.

Gunter, Barrie, David Nicholas and Ian Rowland (2009): *The Google Generation: Are ICT Innovations Changing Information-Seeking Behaviour?* Oxford: Chandor Publishing.

Haddon, Leslie (2004): *Information and Communication Technologies in Everyday Life. A Concise Introduction and Research Guide*. Oxford: Berg Publishers.

Hadenius, Stig, Lennart Weibull and Ingela Wadbring (2008): *Massmedier. Press, radio och TV i den digitala tidsåldern*. Stockholm: Ekerlids förlag.

Halbwachs, Maurice (1950/1980): *The Collective Memory*. New York: Harper & Row.

Halbwachs, Maurice (1992): *On Collective Memory* (Edited, translated and with an introduction by Lewis A. Coser). Chicago & London: University of Chicago Press.

Hall, Stuart (1973): *Encoding/Decoding in the Television Discourse*. Stenciled occasional paper from CCCS no. 7. Birmingham: Birmingham University/CCCS.

Hallin, Daniel and Paolo Mancini (2004): *Comparing Media Systems. Three Models of Media and Politics*. Cambridge: Cambridge University Press.

Hannerz, Ulf (1990): 'Genomsyrade av medier', in Ulf Hannerz (ed.): *Medier och kulturer*. Stockholm: Carlssons, 7–28.

Hareven, Tamara K. (1982): 'The Life Course and Ageing in Historical Perspective', in Tamara K. Hareven and Kathleen J. Adams (eds): *Ageing and Life Course Transitions: An Interdisciplinary Perspective*. New York: Guilford Press.

Hargittai, Eszter (2010): 'Digital Na(t)ives? Variation in Internet Skills and Uses Among Members of the "Net Generation"'. *Sociological Inquiry*, 80(1): 92–113.

Harrington, C. Lee and Denise D. Bielby (1995): *Soap Fans. Pursuing Pleasure and Making Meaning in Everyday Life.* Philadelphia: Temple University Press.

Harrington, C. Lee and Denise D. Bielby (2010): 'A Life Course Perspective on Fandom'. *International Journal of Cultural Studies*, 13(5): 429–50.

Harris, Cheryl and Alison Alexander (ed.) (1998): *Theorizing Fandom. Fans, Subcultures and Identity.* Cresskill, N.J.: Hampton Press.

Hartmann, Maren (2003): *The Web Generation? The (De)construction of Users, Morals and Consumption.* EMTEL2 – Final Report, Brussels: SMIT. Retrieved from www.lse.ac.uk/media@lse/research/EMTEL/reports/hartmann_2003_emtel.pdf. Last accessed 11 March 2015.

Hebdige, Dick (1988): *Hiding in the Light. On Images and Things.* London & New York: Routledge.

Helsper, Ellen Johanna and Rebecca Eynon (2010): 'Digital Natives? Where is the Evidence?'. *British Educational Research Journal*, 36(3): 503–20.

Hepp, Andreas (2013): *Cultures of Mediatization.* Cambridge: Polity Press.

Hepp, Andreas, Matthias Berg and Cindy Roitsch (2014): *Mediatizierte Welten der Vergemeinschaftung: Kommunikative Vernutzung und das Gemeinschaftsleben junger Menschen.* Wiesbaden: Springer Verlag.

Hepp, Andreas, Matthias Berg and Cindy Roitsch (2015): 'Mediengeneration als Prozess: Die mediengenerationelle Selbstpositionierung älterer Menschen'. *Medien & Altern: Zeitschrift für Forschung und Praxis*, 3(6): 19–33.

Hepp, Andreas, Stig Hjarvard and Knut Lundby (2015): 'Mediatization: Theorizing the Interplay between Media, Culture and Society'. *Media, Culture & Society*, 37(2): 314–24.

Hills, Matt (2002): *Fan Cultures.* London & New York: Routledge.

Hjarvard, Stig (2013): *The Mediatization of Culture and Society.* London & New York: Routledge.

Höijer, Birgitta (1998): *Det hörde vi allihopa. Etermedierna och publiken under 1900-talet.* Stockholm: Stiftelsen Etermedierna i Sverige.

Holbrook, Morris B. and Robert M. Schindler (1989): 'Some Exploratory Findings on the Development of Musical Tastes'. *Journal of Consumer Research*, 16(1): 119–24.

Holdsworth, Amy (2011): *Television, Memory and Nostalgia.* Houndmills: Palgrave Macmillan.

Hornby, Nick (1995): *High Fidelity.* New York: Riverhead Books.

Howard, Philip N. (2007): 'Testing the Leap-frog Hypothesis: The Impact of Existing Infrastructure and Telecommunications Policy on the Global Digital Divide'. *Information, Communication & Society*, 10(2): 133–57.

Huang, Hanyun (2014): *Social Media Generation in Urban China: A Study of Social Media Use and Addiction Among Adolescents.* Berlin & Heidelberg: Springer-Verlag.

Hutcheon, Linda (2000): 'Irony, Nostalgia, and the Postmodern'. *Methods for the Study of Literature as Cultural Memory. Studies in Comparative Literature*, 30: 189–207.

International Telecommunication Union (ITU) (2009): *Measuring the Information Society: The ICT Development Index.* Geneva: International Telecommunication Union.

Jaeger, Hans (1985): 'Generations in History: Reflections on a Controversial Concept'. *History and Theory*, 24(3): 273–92.

Jamison, Andrew and Ron Eyerman (1994): *Seeds of the Sixties*, Berkeley & Los Angeles: University of California Press.

Jansen, Bas (2009): 'Tape Cassettes and Former Selves: How Mix Tapes Mediate Memories', in Karin Bijsterveld and José van Dijck (eds): *Sound Souvenirs. Audio Technologies, Memory and Cultural Practices.* Amsterdam: Amsterdam University Press, 43–54.

Jenkins, Henry (2006a): 'Rethinking the Video Game Violence Debate', in David Buckingham and Rebekah Willett (eds): *Digital Generations. Children, Young People, and New Media.* Mahwah, NJ: Lawrence Erlbaum Associates, 19–31.

Jenkins, Henry (2006b): *Fans, Bloggers, and Gamers: Exploring Participatory Culture.* New York: New York University Press.

Jernudd, Åsa (2013): 'Cultural Cinema Memory: National Identity as Expressed by Swedish Elders in an Oral History Project'. *Northern Lights*, 11(1): 109–22.

Jirák, Jan (2006): 'Czech Republic', in Ingrid Volkmer (ed.): *News in Public Memory. An International Study of Media Memories Across Generations.* New York: Peter Lang, 53–68.

Jones, Gill, Anoop Nayak and Brian Davies (2003): 'Review symposium 2: Generations, Culture and Society'. *British Journal of Sociology of Education*, 24(4): 527–34.

Jönsson, Anders and Håkan Jönsson (2014): 'Fyrtiotalisterna och äldreomsorgen: Massmediala konstruktioner av en ny sorts omsorgstagare'. *Sociologisk Forskning*, 51(1): 65–85.

Jordan, Paul (2014): *The Modern Fairy Tale: Nation Branding, National Identity and the Eurovision Song Contest in Estonia.* Tartu: Tartu University Press.

Kalinina, Ekaterina (2014): *Mediated Post-Soviet Nostalgia.* Huddinge: Södertörn University.

Kalmus, Veronika, Margit Keller and Maie Kiisel (2009): 'Emerging Consumer Types in a Transition Culture: Consumption Patterns of Generational and Ethnic Groups in Estonia'. *Journal of Baltic Studies*, 40(1): 53–74.

Kalmus, Veronika, Anu Masso and Marju Lauristin (2013): 'Preferences in Media Use and Perception of Inter-generational Differences among Age Groups in Estonia: A Cultural Approach to Media Generations'. *Northern Lights*, 11(1): 15–34.

Karlsson, Lena (2005): *Klasstillhörighetens subjektiva dimension: Klassidentitet, sociala attityder och fritidsvanor.* Umeå: Umeå Universitet.

Katz, James E., Mark Aakhus, Hyo Dong Kim and Martha Turner (2003): 'Cross-cultural Comparisons of ICTs', in Leopoldina Fortunati, James E. Katz and Raimonda Riccini (eds) *Mediating the Human Body. Technology, Communication, and Fashion.* Mahwah, NJ: Lawrence Erlbaum, 75–86.

Keightley, Emily and Michael Pickering (2012): *The Mnemonic Imagination: Remembering as Creative Practice.* Houndmills: Palgrave Macmillan.

Keller, M. (2005): 'Freedom Calling! Telephony, Mobility and Consumption in Postsocialist Estonia', in *European Journal of Cultural Studies*, 8(2): 217–38.

Kertzer, David I. (1983): 'Generation as a Sociological Problem'. *Annual Review of Sociology*, 9: 125–49.

Kingston, Paul W. (2000): *The Classless Society.* Stanford: Stanford University Press.

Kleberg, Lars (2012): 'Silence and Surveillance. A History of Culture and Communication'. *Baltic Worlds*, 5(1): 18–24.

Kleberg, Madeleine (1994): 'Televisionen flyttar in. En analys av veckopressannonser för TV-apparater kring slutet av 1950-talet', in Ulla Carlsson, Cecilia von Feilitzen, Johan Fornäs, Tove Holmqvist, Sven Ross and Hans Strand (eds): *Kommunikationens korsningar. Möten mellan olika traditioner och perspektiv i medieforskningen.* Göteborg: Nordicom, 163–86.

Kratz, Charlotte (1994): 'Mediemöblemang 1986 och 1993', in Sören Holmberg and Lennart Weibull (eds): *Vägval.* Göteborg: SOM-Institutet, 279–88.

Krotz, Friedrich (2001): *Die Mediatisierung kommunikativen Handelns. Der Wandel von Alltag und sozialen Beziehungen, Kultur und Gesellschaft durch die Medien.* Wiesbaden: Westdeutcher Verlag.

Krotz, Friedric (2007): 'The Meta-process of "Mediatization" as a Conceptual Frame'. *Global Media and Communication*, 3(3): 256–60.

Krumhansl Carol Lynne and Justin Adam Zupnick (2013): Cascading Reminiscence Bumps in Popular Music. *Psychological Science*, 24(10): 2057–68.

Kumar, Keval J., Theo Hug and Gebhard Rusch (2006): 'Construction of Memory', in Ingrid Volkmer (ed.): *News in Public Memory: An International Study of Media Memories Across Generations.* New York: Peter Lang, 211–24.

Laar, Mart (2007): 'The Estonian Economic Miracle'. *Backgrounder,* no. 2060, 1–12, 7 August, Washington: The Heritage Foundation. Available at www.heritage.org/Research/World-wideFreedom/bg2060.cfm. Last accessed 4 April, 2008.

Landsberg, Alison (1995): 'Prosthetic Memory: Total Recall and Blade Runner', in Mike Featherstone and Roger Burrows (eds): *Cyberspace/Cyberbodies/Cyberpunk: Cultures of Technological Embodiment.* London: Sage, 175–90.

Lauk, Epp (1999): 'Practice of Soviet Censorship in the Press: The Case of Estonia'. *Nordicom Review,* 20(2): 19–32.

Lauristin, Marju and Peeter Vihalemm (eds) (1997): *Return to the Western World: Cultural and Political Perspectives on the Estonian Post-Communist Transition.* Tartu: Tartu University Press.

Lefebvre, Henri (1992/2004): *Rhythmanalysis. Space, Time and Everyday Life.* New York: Continuum.

Lepa, Steffen, Anne-Kathrin Hoklas and Stean Weinzierl (2014): 'Discovering and Interpreting Audio Media Generation Units: A Typographical-praxeological Approach to the Mediatization of Everyday Music Listening'. *Participations,* 11(2): 207–38.

Ling, Rich (2004): *The Mobile Connection. The Cell Phone's Impact on Society.* Amsterdam: Morgan Kaufmann.

Livingstone, Sonia (1998): 'Mediated Childhoods: A Comparative Approach to the Lifeworld of Young People in a Changing Media Environment'. *European Journal of Communication,* 13(4): 435–56.

Livingstone, Sonia (2003): 'On the Challenges of Cross-national Comparative Media Research'. *European Journal of Communication,* 18(4): 477–500.

Livingstone, Sonia and Moira Bovill (eds) (2001): *Children and their Changing Media Environment. A European Comparative Study.* Mahwah, NJ & London: Lawrence Earlbaum.

Loos, Eugène, Leslie Haddon and Enid Mante-Meijer (eds) (2012): *Generational Use of New Media.* Farnham: Ashgate.

Lowenthal, David (1985): *The Past is a Foreign Country.* Cambridge: Cambridge University Press.

Lundby, Knut (2008): *Digital Storytelling, Mediatized Stories. Self-Representations in New Media.* New York: Peter Lang.

Lundby, Knut (ed.) (2009a): *Mediatization. Concept, Changes, Consequences.* New York: Peter Lang.

Lundby, Knut (2009b): 'Media Logic: Looking for Social Interaction', in Knut Lundby (ed.): *Mediatization. Concept, Changes, Consequences.* New York: Peter Lang, 101–19.

Lundby, Knut (ed.) (2014): *Mediatization of Communication.* Berlin & Boston: De Gruyter Mouton.

Lundgren, Lars (2012): 'Live from Moscow: The Celebration of Yuri Gagarin and Transnational Television in Europe'. *View: Journal of European Television History and Culture,* 1(2): 45–55.

Lunt, Peter and Sonia Livingstone (2016): 'Is "Mediatization" the New Paradigm for Our Field? A Commentary on Deacon and Stanyer (2014, 2015) and Hepp, Hjarvard and Lundby (2015)'. *Media, Culture & Society,* 38(3): 462–70.

McDaniel, Susan A. (2004): 'Generationing Gender: Justice and the Division of Welfare'. *Journal of Aging Studies,* 19(1): 27–44.

McLuhan, Marshall (1964): *Understanding Media: The Extensions of Man.* New York: McGraw-Hill.

Mannheim, Karl (1928/1952): 'The Problem of Generations', in Karl Mannheim: *Essays in the Sociology of Knowledge.* London: Routledge & Keegan Paul, 276–320.

Mannheim, Karl (1928): 'Das Problem der Generationen'. *Kölner Vierteljahrshefte für Soziologie*, 7: 157-185, 309–30.

Marías, Julián (1961/1970): *Generations: A Historical Method*. Alabama: University of Alabama Press.

Marks, Laura U. (2002): *Touch: Sensuous Theory and Multisensory Media*. Minneapolis: University of Minnesota Press.

Marvin, Carolyn (1988): *When Old Technologies Were New. Thinking about Electric Communication in the Late Nineteenth Century*. New York: Oxford University Press.

Marx, Karl (1852/1995): *The Eighteenth Brumaire of Louis Bonaparte*. Retrieved January 21, 2013, from http://marxists.org/archive/marx/works/1852/18th-brumaire/.

Marx, Karl (1867/1976): *Capital. A Critique of Political Economy*. Volume One, London: Penguin Books.

Mead, Margaret (1970): *Culture and Commitment: A Study of the Generation Gap*. London: Bodley Head.

Mels, Tom (1999): *Wild Landscapes. The Cultural Nature of Swedish National Parks*. Lund: Lund University Press.

Mitchell, W.J. Thomas (ed.)(1994/2002): *Landscape and Power*. Chicago: University of Chicago Press.

Mitterauer, Michael (1986/1991): *Ungdomstidens sociala historia*. Göteborg: Röda Bokförlaget.

Mumford, Lewis (1934/1963): *Technics and Civilization*. New York: Harcourt, Brace and World.

Mumford, Lewis (1967): *The Myth of the Machine: Technics and Human Development*. Vol. 1. New York: Harcourt, Brace, Jovanovich.

Murdock, Graham and Robin McCron (1976): 'Consciousness of Class and Consciousness of Generation', in Stuart Hall and Tony Jefferson (eds): *Resistance Through Rituals. Youth Sub-cultures in Post-war Britain*. London: HarperCollins, 192–207.

Närvänen, Anna-Liisa and Elisabet Näsman (2004): 'Childhood as Generation or Life Phase?' *Young*, 12(1): 71–91.

Niemeyer, Katharina (2014a): 'Introduction: Media and Nostalgia', in Katharina Niemeyer (ed.): *Media and Nostalgia: Yearning for the Past, Present and Future*. Houndmills: Palgrave Macmillan, 1–23.

Niemeyer, Katharina (ed.) (2014b): *Media and Nostalgia: Yearning for the Past, Present and Future*. Houndmills: Palgrave Macmillan.

Nowak, Kjell (1996): 'Medier som materiell och mental miljö', in Ulla Carlsson (ed.): *Medierna i samhället: Igår, idag, imorgon*. Göteborg: Nordicom, 159–76.

Nowak, Kjell (1999): 'Medieutvecklingen och vardagen', in Ulla Carlsson (ed.): *Medierna i samhället. Kontinuitet och förändring*. Göteborg: Nordicom, 65–8.

Nyre, Lars (2009): *Sound Media: From Live Journalism to Music Recording*. London & New York: Routledge.

O'Donnell, Mike (2010): 'Generation and Utopia: Using Mannheim's Concepts to Understand 1960s Radicalism'. *Young*, 18(4): 367–83.

Ong, Walter (1967): *The Presence of the Word: Some Prolegomena for the Cultural and Religious History*. Minneapolis: University of Minnesota Press.

Opermann, Signe (2013): 'Understanding Changing News Media Use: Generations and their Media Vocabulary'. *Northern Lights*, 11(1): 123–46.

Opermann, Signe (2014): *Generational Use of News Media in Estonia: Media Access, Spatial Orientations and Discursive Characteristics of the News Media*. Huddinge: Södertörn University.

Ortega y Gasset, José (1923/1931): *The Modern Theme*. London: The C. W. Daniel company.

Ortega y Gasset, José (1930/1932): *The Revolt of the Masses*. New York: W.W. Norton & Co.

Parks, Lisa (2012): 'Technostruggles and the Satellite Dish: A Populist Approach to Infrastructure', in Göran Bolin (ed.): *Cultural Technologies. The Shaping of Culture in Media and Society*. New York: Routledge, 64–86.

Parks, Lisa (2015): '"Stuff You Can Kick": Toward a Theory of Media Infrastructures', in Patrik Svensson and David Theo Goldberg (eds): *Between Humanities and the Digital*. Cambridge, MA: MIT Press, 355–73.

Pearson, Roberta (ed.) (2009): *Reading Lost: Perspectives on a Hit Television Show*. London: I.B. Taurus.

Philips, James (1985): 'Distance, Absence, and Nostalgia', in Don Ihde and Hugh J. Silverman (eds), *Descriptions*. Albany: State University of New York Press, 64–75.

Pickering, Michael and Emily Keightley (2014): 'Retrotyping and the Marketing of Nostalgia', in Katharina Niemeyer (ed.): *Media and Nostalgia: Yearning for the Past, Present and Future*. Houndmills: Palgrave Macmillan, 83–95.

Pilcher, Jane (1994): 'Mannheim's Sociology of Generations: An Undervalued Legacy'. *The British Journal of Sociology*, 45(3): 481–95.

Pilcher, Jane (1998): *Women of their Time: Generation, Gender Issues and Feminism*. Aldershot: Ashgate.

Pinch, Trevor and David Reinecke (2009): 'Technostalgia: How Old Gear Lives on in New Music', in Karin Bijsterveld and José van Dijck (eds): *Sound Souvenirs. Audio Technologies, Memory and Cultural Practices*. Amsterdam: Amsterdam University Press, 152–66.

Pinder, Wilhelm (1926): *Das Problem der Generation in der Kunstgeschichte Europas*. Berlin: Frankfurter Verlags-Anstalt.

Ponte, Christina and Piermarco Aroldi (2013): 'Conectando generaciones: Investigación y aprendizaje en educación en medios y estudios de audiencia'. *Comunicar*. 21(41): 167–76.

Prensky, Mark (2001): *Digital Games-based Learning*. New York: McGraw-Hill.

Proust, Marcel (1913/1996): *In Search of Lost Time. Vol. 1: Swann's Way*. London: Vintage.

Rantanen, Terhi (2005): *The Media and Globalization*. London: Sage.

Renberg, Tore (2015): 'Thåström hällde bensin på bålet'. *Dagens Nyheter* 8 February 2015. Available at www.dn.se/kultur-noje/musik/thastrom-hallde-bensin-pa-balet/. Last accessed 8 February 2015.

Ricoeur, Paul (1985/1990): *Time and Narrative. Volume 3*. Chicago & London: The University of Chicago Press.

Rogers, Everett M. (2003): *The Diffusion of Innovations*. New York: Free Press.

Roomets, Echo (2013): 'Vikerraadio õhtujutt kestab seni, kuni Eestis lapsi sünnib'. *Õhtoleht*, 31 August 2013. Available at www.ohtuleht.ee/539958/vikerraadio-ohtujutt-kestab-seni-kuni-eestis-lapsi-sunnib. Last accessed 23 November 2015.

Rosa, Hartmut (2005/2013): *Social Acceleration: A New Theory of Modernity*. New York: Columbia University Press.

Rubin David C., Tamara A. Rahhal and Leonard W. Poon (1998): 'Things Learned in Early Adulthood are Remembered Best'. *Memory & Cognition*, 26(1): 3–19.

Rubin David C., Scott E. Wetzler and Robert D. Nebes (1986): 'Autobiographical Memory Across the Lifespan', in David C. Rubin (ed.): *Autobiographical Memory*. Cambridge: Cambridge University Press, 202–21.

Runnel, Pille, Pille Pruulmann-Vengerfeldt and Margit Keller (2006): 'A Mobile Phone Isn't a Mobile Phone Anymore', in Fay Sudweeks, Herbert Hrachovec and Charles Ess (eds): *Proceedings, Cultural Attitudes towards Communication and Technology 2006*. Perth: Murdoch University, 606–21.

Runnel, Pille, Pille Pruulmann-Vengerfeldt and Kristina Reinsalu (2009): 'The Estonian Tiger Leap from Post-communism to the Information Society'. *Journal of Baltic Studies*, 40(1): 29–51.

Ryder, Norman B. (1965): 'The Cohort as a Concept in the Study of Social Change'. *American Sociological Review*, 30(6): 843–61.

Schuman, Howard and Amy Corning (2014): 'Collective Memory and Autobiographical Memory: Similar but not the Same'. *Memory Studies*, 7(2): 146–60.

Schutz, Alfred (1967): *The Phenomenology of the Social World*. Evanston, IL: Northwestern University Press.

Siibak, Andra and Virge Tamme (2013): '"Who Introduced Granny to Facebook?"' An Exploration of Everyday Family Interactions in Web-based Communication Environments'. *Northern Lights*, 11(1): 71–89.

Siibak, Andra and Nicoletta Vittadini (2012). 'Introducing Four Empirical Examples of the "Generationing" Process'. *Cyberpsychology: Journal of Psychosocial Research on Cyberspace*, 6(2): 1-10. doi: 10.5817/CP201221.

Siibak, Andra, Nicoloetta Vittadini and Galit Nimrod (2014): 'Generations as Media Audiences: An Introduction'. *Participations*, 11(2): 100–7.

Silverstone, Roger, Eric Hirsch and David Morley (1992): 'Information and Communication Technologies and the Moral Economy of the Household', in Roger Silverstone and Eric Hirsch (eds) *Consuming Technologies: Media and Information in Domestic Spaces*. London: Routledge, 15–31.

Sontag, Susan (1977): *On Photography*. New York: Farrar, Straus & Giroux.

Spigel, Lynn (1992): *Make Room for TV. Television and the Family Ideal in Postwar America*. Chicago & London: University of Chicago Press.

Spitzer, Alan B. (1973): 'The Historical Problem of Generation'. *The American Historical Review*, 78(5): 1353–85.

Steiner, Kristina L., David B. Pillemer, Dorthe Kirkegaard Thomsen and Andrew P. Minigan (2014): 'The Reminiscence Bump in Older Adults' Life Story Transitions'. *Memory*, 22(8): 1002-9. DOI: 10.1080/09658211.2013.863358.

Stevens, Catherine J. (2015): 'Is Memory for Music Special?' *Memory Studies*, 8(3): 263–6.

Strauss, William and Neil Howe (1991): *Generations: The History of America's Future, 1584–2069*. New York: William Morrow & Company.

Sūna, Laura (2013): '"Senior Pop Music?" The Role of Folk-like Schlager Music for Elderly People'. *Northern Lights*, 11(1): 91–108.

Taipale, Sakari (2016): 'Synchronicity Matters: Defining the Characteristics of Digital Generations'. *Information, Communication & Society*, 19(1): 80–94.

Tapscott, Don (1998): *Growing Up Digital: The Rise of the Net Generation*. New York: McGraw-Hill.

Teer-Tomaselli, Ruth (2006): 'Memory and Markers: Collective Memories and Newsworthyness', in Ingrid Volkmer (ed.): *News in Public Memory: An International Study of Media Memories Across Generations*. New York: Peter Lang, 225–49.

ter Bogt, Tom F.M., Marc J.W.H. Diesling, Maarten van Zalk, Peter G. Christenson and Wim H.J. Meeus (2011): 'Intergenerational Continuity of Taste: Parental and Adolescent Music Preferences'. *Social Forces*, 90(1): 297–319.

Turner, Bryan S. (2002): 'Strategic Generations: Historical Change, Literary Expression, and Generational Politics', in June Edmunds and Bryan S. Turner (eds): *Generational Consciousness, Narrative and Politics*. Lanham, Boulder, New York & Oxford: Rowman & Littlefield, 13–29.

Twenge, Jean M. (2006): *Generation Me: Why Today's Young Americans Are More Confident, Assertive, Entitled – And More Miserable Than Ever Before*. New York: Free Press.

Vagliasindi, Maria, Izzet Güney and Chris Taubman (2006): 'Fixed and Mobile Competition in Transition Economies'. *Telecommunications Policy*, 30(7): 349–67.

van Dijck, José (2009): 'Remembering Songs through Telling Stories: Pop Music as Resource', in Karin Bijsterveld and José van Dijck (eds), *Sound Souvenirs. Audio Technologies, Memory and Cultural Practices*. Amsterdam: Amsterdam University Press, 107–22.

Vanden Abeele, Mariek, Marjolijn L. Antheunis and Alexander P. Schouten (2014): 'Me, Myself and My Mobile: A Segmentation of Youths Based on Their Attitudes towards the Mobile Phone as a Status Instrument'. *Telematics and Informatics*, 31(2): 194–208.

Vincent, John A. (2005): 'Understanding Generations: Political Economy and Culture in an Ageing Society'. *The British Journal of Sociology*, 56(4): 579–99.

Vittadini, Nicoletta, Daniele Milese and Piermarco Aroldi (2013a): 'New-generation Ties: Identity, Social Relations and Digital Technologies among 2G Migrants in Italy', *Observatorio (OBS*) Journal* (Special issue), 61–88.

Vittadini, Nicoletta, Andra Siibak, Irena Reifová, and Helena Bilandzic (2013b): 'Generations and Media: The Social Construction of Generational Identity and Differences', in Nico Carpentier, Kim Christian Schrøder and Lawrie Hallet (eds.) *Audience Transformations. Shifting Audience Positions in Late Modernity*. New York and London: Routledge, 65–81.

Volkmer, Ingrid (ed.) (2006a): *News in Public Memory. An International Study of Media Memories across Generations*. New York: Peter Lang.

Volkmer, Ingrid (2006b): 'Globalisation, Generational Entelechies, and the Global Public Space', in Ingrid Volkmer (ed.): *News in Public Memory. An International Study of Media Memories across Generations*. New York: Peter Lang, 251–68.

Wickström, David-Emil and Yngvar B. Steinholt (2009): 'Visions of the (Holy) Motherland in Contemporary Russian Popular Music: Nostalgia, Patriotism, Religion and *Russkii Rok*'. *Popular Music & Society*, 32(3): 313–30.

Williams, Raymond (1961/1965): *The Long Revolution*. Harmondsworth: Penguin.

Winston, Brian (1998): *Media Technology and Society. A History: From the Telegraph to the Internet*. London & New York: Routledge.

Wrong, Dennis H. (1994): *The Problem of Order. What Unites and Divides Society*. New York: The Free Press.

Wyatt, David (1993): *Out of the Sixties. Storytelling and the Vietnam Generation*. Cambridge: Cambridge University Press.

Ziehe, Thomas and Herbert Stubenrauch (1982): *Plädoyer für ungewöhnliches Lernen. Ideen zur Jugendsituation*. Hamburg: Rowohlt

Zimmermann, Patricia R. (1995): *Reel Families: A Social History of Amateur Film*. Bloomington & Indianapolis: Indiana University Press.

Zukin, Cliff, Scott Keeter, Molly Andolina, Krista Jenkins and Michael X. Delli Carpini (2006): *A New Engagement? Political Participation, Civic Life, and the Changing American Citizen*. New York: Oxford University Press.

INDEX